Facts about Fast Food

Compare the fat, calories, and sodium for these fast-food favorites to the healthier counterpart recipes in this book. In most cases, you can have dinner on the table in less time than it takes to go through the drive-through window.

Restaurant	Menu Item Instead try:	Calories	Fat (g)	Sodium (mg)
McDonald's®	Big Mac®	560	31	1070
	Turkey Patties with Piquant Sauce (page 123)	**177**	**4.5**	**69**
McDonald's®	Arch Deluxe™	550	31	1070
	Beef Patties with Sweet-and-Sour Onions (page 89)	**226**	**5.9**	**68**
Burger King®	Hamburger	330	15	530
	Turkey Patties with Piquant Sauce (page 123)	**177**	**4.5**	**69**
Arby's®	Regular roast beef	388	19	1009
	Roast Beef-Feta Pita Pockets (page 149)	**187**	**4.3**	**821**
Taco Bell®	Taco salad with salsa	850	52	1780
	Beef Salad Olé (page 135)	**263**	**5.7**	**968**
Wendy's®	Grilled chicken sandwich	310	8	790
	Grilled Chicken and Raspberry Salad (page 136)	**238**	**3.9**	**81**
KFC®	Original Recipe® chicken breast	400	24	1116
	Grilled Herbed Chicken (page 104)	**144**	**3.5**	**62**
Wendy's®	Broccoli and cheese potato	470	14	470
	Primavera Stuffed Potatoes (page 66)	**319**	**4.2**	**813**
Taco Bell®	Veggie Fajita Wrap™	420	19	980
	Garden Vegetable Wraps (page 145)	**194**	**6.1**	**461**

**Grouper with Honey
Citrus Glaze**
(recipe, page 49)

Vegetable-Cheese Pizza
(recipe, page 64)

Fig and Blue Cheese Salad
(recipe, page 131)

French Onion Sandwiches
(recipe, page 144)

Weight Watchers.

15·Minute
Cookbook

Oxmoor
House.

Library of Congress Catalog Card Number: 98-67730
ISBN: 0-8487-1822-4
Manufactured in the United States of America
Second Printing 1999

Be sure to check with your health-care provider before making any changes in your diet.

Weight Watchers is a registered trademark of Weight Watchers International, Inc., and is used under license by Healthy Living, Inc.

Editor-in-Chief: Nancy Fitzpatrick Wyatt
Senior Foods Editor: Katherine M. Eakin
Senior Editor, Editorial Services: Olivia Kindig Wells
Art Director: James Boone

Weight Watchers 15-Minute Cookbook

Editor: Deborah Garrison Lowery
Foods Editor: Anne Chappell Cain, M.S., M.P.H., R.D.
Associate Art Director: Cynthia R. Cooper
Designer: Clare T. Minges
Copy Editor: Donna Baldone
Editorial Assistant: Catherine Ritter Scholl
Director, Test Kitchens: Kathleen Royal Phillips
Assistant Director, Test Kitchens: Gayle Hays Sadler
Test Kitchens Staff: Susan Hall Bellows, Julie Christopher, Natalie E. King, Andrea Noble,
     Iris Crawley O'Brien, Alyson Pride, Jan A. Smith
Recipe Developers: Margaret Chason Agnew, Beth Allen, Caroline A. Grant, Elizabeth Tyler Luckett,
     Debby Maugans Nakos, Lisa Hooper Talley
Photographer: Brit Huckabay
Photo Stylist: Virginia Cravens
Publishing Systems Administrator: Rick Tucker
Director, Production and Distribution: Phillip Lee
Associate Production Manager: Vanessa Cobbs Richardson
Production Assistant: Faye Porter Bonner

We're Here for You!

We at Oxmoor House are dedicated to serving you with reliable information that expands your imagination and enriches your life. We welcome your comments and suggestions. Please write us at:

Oxmoor House, Inc.
Editor, *Weight Watchers*
     15-Minute Cookbook
2100 Lakeshore Drive
Birmingham, AL 35209

To order additional publications, call
1-205-877-6560.

Cover: Cranberry-Apricot Chicken, page 106
Back Cover: Garden Vegetable Wraps, page 145

CONTENTS

Introduction

Weight Watchers Recipes

Top 10 Secrets of a Fast Food Pro

If your lifestyle dictates quick, get-it-on-the-table meals,
these 10 tips will make you an expert in superfast cooking.

1: Go Ahead and Ask

Quiz family members about their favorite recipes, even if you already know what they like. They'll love having input.

2: Stock Up on Staples

List the foods and seasonings your family loves, and have them on hand. Keep a copy of the list for restocking.

3: Organize for Speed

You'll be a speed demon in the kitchen if you store things such as mixing bowls, pot holders, spices, and knives where you use them.

4: Go Tool Shopping

Tools for low-fat speed cooking include a nonstick skillet, two or three saucepans, a steamer basket, a broiling pan with a rack, good sharp knives, and kitchen scissors.

Kitchen scissors probably are the most helpful for saving preparation time. Use them for chopping cooked chicken, trimming the fat from meat, chopping fresh herbs over a measuring cup, and cutting dried fruit. Using scissors also saves washing a cutting board.

5: Try Just One

Pick just one new recipe to try instead of several for a single meal. Try an entrée; then serve easy standby recipes for side dishes, or pick up the side dishes and bread at the grocery deli.

6: Think Ahead

Planning will save you time. No more worrying about the menu as you fight 5 o'clock traffic, or scrounging in the fridge to see what you can cook. In the morning put dinner on in the slow cooker. Or try out the menu ideas included with each recipe in this book. Better yet, let each family member plan one meal a week.

7: Go for Ease

Convenience products such as frozen chopped meats and vegetables and canned seasoned vegetable blends save cooking and cleanup time. Look for produce sliced or chopped the way you plan to use it; you'll find the packages in the produce section or pre-cut vegetables in the grocery deli or on the salad bar.

One of the handiest new frozen products on the market is called "seasoning blend." This package of chopped peppers, onions, celery, and parsley is found in the frozen food section of the supermarket.

Don't forget ready-to-serve pizza crusts; deli-roasted chicken; peeled, cooked shrimp; and spice blends.

8: Do Double Duty

Cook something that requires attention while another recipe simmers or bakes. For example, put on rice to cook before you start cooking the entrée, or chop vegetables while something else simmers.

9: Beg, Plead, or Delegate

Or do whatever it takes to get help in the kitchen before and after mealtime. Even 3-year-olds can set out the napkins, and the older kids can pour the beverages, set the table, or stir a sauce. Don't forget to encourage help with the cleanup, too.

10: Wipe Out Cleanup

The best way to cut down on cleanup is not to have to do it at all. See the box below for three of the easiest ways to prevent unnecessary cleanup.

Quick Cleanup Cures

Save yourself time with these three easy steps for cleanup prevention.

1. Use vegetable cooking spray.
• Baked food won't be as hard to clean off casserole dishes and pans if you coat them first.
• Spray kitchen scissors before chopping sticky ingredients such as dried fruit.
• Coat measuring cups and spoons before measuring a sticky ingredient like honey, and the honey will slide out easily. (Rinsing measuring cups with cold water before measuring sticky ingredients works, too.)

2. Measure and mix ingredients with cleanup in mind.
• For instance, if the recipe calls for beaten eggs, beat them first in the bowl; then add other ingredients to save cleaning a bowl.
• Or measure dry ingredients before wet ones, and you won't have to wash measuring utensils in between measurings.
• Chop dry or less messy ingredients in the food processor before mixing wet mixtures, and you won't have to wash the processor bowl but once.

3. Use throw-away paper products when possible.
• Measure ingredients on waxed paper.
• Line baking pans with aluminum foil.
• Skim fat from gravy by using a heavy-duty zip-top plastic bag; pour the broth into the bag, and seal. Any fat will quickly float to the top. Snip a hole (with kitchen scissors, of course) in one corner to allow the broth or gravy to flow into a measuring cup. Pinch closed the hole just before the fat begins to leave the bag; then you can throw away the bag and remaining fat.
• Melt chocolate morsels in a heavy-duty zip-top plastic bag. Seal the bag, and place it in a saucepan of hot water until the chocolate melts. Snip a tiny hole in one corner of the bag to squeeze out the melted chocolate.

About These Recipes

Weight Watchers® 15-Minute Cookbook gives you the nutrition facts you want to know. To make your life easier, we've provided the following useful information with every recipe:

- Diabetic exchange values for those who use them as a guide for planning meals
- A number calculated through **POINTS®** Food System, an integral part of *Weight Watchers* **1•2•3 Success**™ Weight Loss Plan
- A complete nutrient analysis per serving

Diabetic Exchanges

Exchange values are provided for people who use them for calorie-controlled diets and for people with diabetes. All foods within a certain group contain approximately the same amount of nutrients and calories, so one serving of a food from a food group can be substituted or exchanged for one serving of any other item on the list.

The food groups are meat, starch, fruit, vegetable, fat, and milk. The exchange values are based on the *Exchange Lists for Meal Planning* developed by the American Diabetes Association and The American Dietetic Association.

POINTS Food System

Every recipe in the book also includes a number assigned through **POINTS.** This system uses a formula based on the calorie, fat, and fiber content of the food. Foods with more calories and fat (like a slice of pepperoni pizza) receive high numbers, while fruits and vegetables receive low numbers. For more information about the numbers assigned through **POINTS,** the

1•2•3 Success Weight Loss Plan, and the *Weight Watchers* meeting nearest you, call 1-800-651-6000.

Nutritional Analyses

Each recipe offers a complete listing of nutrients; the numbers in the list are based on the following assumptions:

- Unless otherwise indicated, meat, poultry, and fish refer to skinned, boned, and cooked servings.
- When we give a range for an ingredient (3 to 3½ cups flour, for instance), we calculate using the lesser amount.
- Some alcohol calories evaporate during heating; the analysis reflects that.
- Only the amount of marinade absorbed by the food is used in calculation.
- Garnishes and optional ingredients are not included in analysis.

The nutritional values used in our calculations either come from a computer program by Computrition, Inc., or are provided by food manufacturers.

just the basics

Just the Basics

Call this chapter a primer for The Can't-Boil-Water Cook. The Fabulous-But-Forgetful Cook will love it as a reference. It's a great introduction for The Learning-to-Cook-Light Cook. And The Inspired Cook will read it for great ideas.

If any of the above sounds like you, you'll find "Just the Basics" to be a handy companion to the recipe chapters in this book. The key to quick cooking is knowing what to do with ingredients you have on hand, and being able to memorize or quick-reference basic cooking information that most cookbooks take for granted you know.

For instance, if the recipe calls for chopped cooked chicken, you can turn to our instructions for poaching or roasting boneless chicken breasts (opposite page). You'll have chopped cooked chicken in just 10 minutes.

Or if the menu suggestion includes serving the recipe with steamed asparagus, find out what to do from the vegetable steaming chart (page 19).

Here's a sample of other how-tos you'll find on the next few pages:

- Trendy, but easy, low-fat ways to add flavor, like cooking rice in broth and roasting vegetables.

- Three ways to toast nuts in 5 minutes or less.

- The trick to preparing a 10-minute baked potato.

- The simplest way to roast a turkey breast in just 1½ hours.

- A catchy formula for cooking rice. You'll never have to look up the instructions and measurements on the bag again.

- A guide for deciding how much pasta to cook.

So keep this chapter handy, and the answers to your cooking questions will be at your fingertips.

Cooked Chicken

When the recipe calls for chopped cooked chicken, here are two
ways to cook plain, but tender and juicy, chicken breasts.

Skillet-Poached Chicken

What you'll need:

Large skillet or saucepan

Liquid (water, apple juice, wine, or
    no-salt-added chicken broth)

Herbs and spices (optional)

Boneless, skinless chicken breast halves

What to do:

1. In a large skillet or saucepan, add enough
water or liquid to cover chicken. (Do not add
chicken at this point.) Add herbs, if desired.

2. Bring water or other liquid to a boil;
reduce heat to low, and add chicken. Cover
and simmer 12 minutes or until chicken is tender (smaller breast halves will cook more
quickly). Do not overcook the chicken or it
will be tough.

Oven-Roasted Chicken

What you'll need:

Boneless, skinless chicken breast halves

Large jelly roll pan

Vegetable cooking spray

What to do:

1. Place boneless, skinless chicken breast halves
on a jellyroll pan coated with vegetable cooking spray. Bake at 450° for 10 to 15 minutes or
until juices run clear and chicken is done.

How to Shred Chicken

You need only two forks to shred
chicken into long strands. Just hold
one fork in each hand and use the
tines like scissors to pull through
the chicken in opposite directions.
Chicken shreds more easily while it's
still warm.

Roasted Turkey Breast

You can bake a turkey breast in about one-third the time it takes to bake an entire turkey. Here's a no-mess way to do it.

What you'll need:

1 (4-pound) turkey breast, skinned
1 medium onion, halved (optional)
2 stalks celery, halved (optional)
Vegetable cooking spray
Meat thermometer
Oven cooking bag
Large baking pan

What to do:

1. Trim fat from turkey breast. Rinse turkey breast thoroughly under cold water, and pat dry with paper towels. Place onion and celery in turkey breast cavity; spray turkey with cooking spray.

2. Insert meat thermometer into thickest part of turkey, making sure it does not touch bone. (If you use an instant-read thermometer, it does not need to be inserted in turkey throughout cooking time.)

3. Place turkey in an oven cooking bag; secure bag with twist tie. Place turkey, meaty side up, in a baking pan. Bake at 325° for 1 hour. Cut a slit in top of bag; bake 30 additional minutes or until meat thermometer registers 170°.

4. Transfer turkey to a serving platter; remove and discard onion and celery. Let turkey stand 15 minutes before slicing. Yield: 10 servings.

Turkey Tips for Saving Time and Reducing Fat

Cooking the turkey with the skin removed helps reduce the fat, and using an oven cooking bag keeps the meat moist and juicy.

Serve the best slices for dinner or save them for sandwiches. Freeze the remaining meat in heavy-duty, zip-top plastic bags for casseroles and stews.

To get more meat off the bone after slicing, place the turkey breast in a large Dutch oven, and cover with water. Simmer, covered, 30 minutes to 1 hour. You'll find that the remaining meat comes off the bone more easily.

You'll also have some delicious low-sodium turkey broth to strain and use as poaching liquid, as a base for soup, or for cooking rice. Just freeze the broth in 1- or 2-cup portions to thaw and use when you need it.

Basic Rice

Cooking rice is easy as 1-2-3. Remember this easy formula:
1 cup rice + 2 cups water = 3 cups cooked rice.

What you'll need:

2 cups water
Medium saucepan
1 cup uncooked long-grain rice

What to do:

1. Bring water to a boil in a medium saucepan; add rice. Cover, reduce heat to low, and simmer 20 minutes or until water is absorbed and rice is tender. Yield: 3 cups.

Ten-Minute Rice

Success and Uncle Ben's now make quick-cooking rice; it cooks in just 10 minutes. The rice comes premeasured in bags—all you do is drop the bag in boiling water, cover, and simmer. Regular-size bags of quick-cooking rice make 2 cups of cooked rice. New larger bags make 3 cups of cooked rice.

Basic Pasta

What you'll need:

3 quarts water per 8 ounces uncooked pasta
Large saucepan, Dutch oven, or stockpot
Pasta

What to do:

1. Bring water to a boil in a large saucepan, Dutch oven, or stockpot; add pasta. To add long pasta to boiling water, hold pasta by the handful with one set of ends in the boiling water, and push gently, until it softens enough to submerge.

2. Cook pasta, uncovered, in boiling water for length of time indicated on the package for specific type of pasta, usually 8 to 10 minutes.

3. Just before end of cooking time, check to see if pasta is pliable but firm, and no longer starchy. (If pasta will be cooked further in a casserole, slightly undercook it to keep it from being mushy.)

How Much Pasta Do You Need?

You can substitute pastas of similar sizes and shapes (such as macaroni for penne or linguine for spaghetti) if you measure it by weight rather than in cups. Use this guide to determine how much to cook.

Linguine, Spaghetti, or Vermicelli:
4 ounces dry = 2 to 3 cups cooked
8 ounces dry = 4 to 5 cups cooked
16 ounces dry = 8 to 9 cups cooked

Macaroni, Penne, or Rotini:
4 ounces dry = 2½ cups cooked
8 ounces dry = 4½ cups cooked

Baked Potatoes/Baked Sweet Potatoes

What you'll need:

Baking potatoes or sweet potatoes
Vegetable cooking spray (optional)
Pot holder

What to do:

1. Wash potatoes, and pat dry with paper towels. For softer skins, coat potatoes with cooking spray, if desired.

2. Place potatoes directly on the rack of oven. Bake baking potatoes at 400° and sweet potatoes at 375° for 1 hour or until done. To check for doneness, use a potholder to squeeze one potato at a time. Potatoes are done when sides "give" and seem soft.

Baked Potatoes in Minutes

When there's no time to waste, throw a potato in the microwave, and it's ready to eat in about 10 minutes. First rinse medium-size (about 6- to 7-ounce) potatoes, and prick the skin with a fork to keep the potatoes from exploding as they cook. Arrange the potatoes in a circle, end to end. Microwave at HIGH, turning and re-arranging the potatoes once, and using the following times. Let the potatoes stand 5 minutes after cooking.

• • •

Number of Potatoes	Minutes at HIGH
1	4 to 6
2	7 to 8
3	9 to 11
4	12 to 14
5	16 to 18

Roasted Vegetables

Cooking vegetables in the oven at a high temperature or "roasting" is an easy, low-fat way to get intense, sweet vegetable flavor quickly. Roast root vegetables such as carrots, potatoes, parsnips, turnips, and onions together, since they take longer to cook than other vegetables.

What you'll need:

Vegetables such as carrots, corn, eggplant, mushrooms, onions, parsnips, peppers, potatoes, squash, and turnips

Sharp knife

Vegetable cooking spray

Shallow roasting pan or baking sheet (heavier ones are best)

What to do:

1. Cut vegetables into uniform-size pieces; coat with cooking spray.

2. Place vegetables in a single layer in a shallow roasting pan coated with cooking spray. Do not crowd vegetables. Bake at 425° for 15 to 20 minutes for carrots, parsnips, potatoes, onions, and turnips, and 10 to 15 minutes for most other vegetables, stirring occasionally.

Watch Out for Fat!

If you're ordering roasted vegetables at a restaurant or from the supermarket takeout, don't assume they're as low in fat as those roasted by the method on this page. Many chefs add olive oil in hefty amounts for flavor. If in doubt, just ask your waiter how the vegetables are roasted. Then opt for steamed veggies if the roasted ones are coated in oil.

Steamed Vegetables

Steaming is one of the quickest, healthiest ways to cook vegetables.

What you'll need:

Saucepan, wok, or Dutch oven with
  tight-fitting lid
Steaming basket or rack that sits above 1-inch
  water level
Vegetables

What to do:

1. Place at least 1 inch of water in the bottom of a saucepan, wok, or Dutch oven; insert steamer basket or rack. Place over high heat, and bring water to a boil.

2. Add vegetables, cover, and return water to a boil. Reduce heat to low, and allow water to simmer for recommended time or until vegetables are tender. Add boiling water to pan during cooking, if necessary.

Vegetable	Preparation	Steaming Time
Asparagus	Snap off tough ends of asparagus. Remove scales with a vegetable peeler, if desired.	8 to 10 minutes
Beans, green	Wash; trim ends, and remove strings. Leave whole or cut into 1½-inch pieces.	10 minutes
Broccoli	Remove outer leaves and tough ends of lower stalks. Wash; cut into spears.	10 to 12 minutes
Brussels sprouts	Wash; remove discolored leaves. Cut off stem ends; slash bottoms with "X."	10 minutes
Carrots	Scrape; remove ends, and rinse. Leave tiny carrots whole; slice large carrots or cut into strips.	4 to 8 minutes
Cauliflower	Remove outer leaves and stalk. Wash and break into flowerets.	10 to 12 minutes
Peas, snow	Wash; trim ends, and remove tough strings.	2 to 4 minutes
Potatoes, round red	Scrub; peel a strip from around center.	10 to 20 minutes
Squash, summer	Wash; trim ends. Slice or cut into strips.	10 to 12 minutes

Toasted Nuts

Heating pecans, almonds, and walnuts until just darkened and toasted adds a rich, more pronounced flavor. Use one of the three toasting methods below.

What you'll need:

Shallow baking dish, shallow baking pan, or
    heavy skillet
Large spoon
¼ cup nuts

What to do:

Microwave Method: Spread nuts in a single layer in a shallow baking dish. Microwave at HIGH 2 to 4 minutes, stopping every 30 seconds to stir and sample the nuts since nuts may burn quickly. Microwave longer for more nuts.

Oven Method: Spread nuts in a single layer in a shallow baking pan. Bake at 350° for 10 to 15 minutes or until nuts are toasted, stirring occasionally.

Skillet Method: Place a heavy skillet over high heat. Add nuts, and cook 1 to 2 minutes, stirring often, until nuts are toasted.

More Flavor, Less Fat

In low-fat recipes, the key is to use only a few nuts for texture and taste to keep the fat low. When the nuts are toasted, the flavor boost makes it seem as if there are more of them. Also if you chop the nuts coarsely you get a bigger taste of nut flavor in each bite than if you chop them finely.

Peach Melba Brûlée
(recipe, page 31)

Mixed Berry Dessert
(recipe, page 24)

desserts

Mixed Berry Dessert (photo, page 22)

EXCHANGES

1 Fruit

POINTS

1

PER SERVING

106 Calories
20.0g Carbohydrate
0.3g Fat (0.0g saturated)
4.6g Fiber
0.5g Protein
0mg Cholesterol
8mg Sodium
15mg Calcium
0.3mg Iron

3	tablespoons Grand Marnier or other orange-flavored liqueur
½	teaspoon grated fresh orange rind
1	tablespoon sugar
1	cup fresh blueberries
1	cup fresh blackberries or raspberries
½	cup frozen fat-free whipped topping, thawed

Orange curls or grated orange rind (optional)

1. Combine first 3 ingredients in a medium bowl, stirring until sugar dissolves. Add blueberries and blackberries, tossing gently.

2. Spoon mixture into individual dessert dishes. Top each serving with 2 tablespoons whipped topping. If desired, garnish with orange curls or orange rind. Yield: 4 (½-cup) servings.

Serve with shrimp pasta salad and fresh tomato slices.

For a nonalcoholic version, substitute orange juice for Grand Marnier.

Caramelized Orange Bananas

2   large bananas
1½   teaspoons reduced-calorie margarine
¼   cup firmly packed brown sugar
¼   cup unsweetened orange juice
⅛   to ¼ teaspoon banana extract
2   cups vanilla nonfat ice cream

1. Peel bananas, and cut each in half. Cut banana halves lengthwise into quarters; set aside.

2. Add margarine to a medium skillet, and place over medium heat until margarine melts. Stir in brown sugar, and cook, stirring constantly, until sugar dissolves and mixture begins to bubble. Stir in orange juice, and add bananas to skillet. Increase heat to medium-high, and cook 2 minutes, stirring gently. Turn bananas, and sprinkle with banana extract.

3. Spoon ½ cup ice cream into each of four individual dessert bowls; spoon warm bananas evenly over ice cream. Serve immediately. Yield: 4 servings.

Serve with grilled pork tenderloin, steamed asparagus, and glazed baby carrots.

Here's a rich-tasting dessert that will remind you of Bananas Foster. This nonalcoholic version doesn't require flaming.

EXCHANGES
1 Starch
2 Fruit

POINTS
4

PER SERVING
199 Calories
45.1g Carbohydrate
1.2g Fat (0.1g saturated)
1.6g Fiber
2.7g Protein
0mg Cholesterol
58mg Sodium
12mg Calcium
0.4mg Iron

Island Fruit Dessert

EXCHANGES

1 Starch

1½ Fruit

½ Fat

POINTS

4

2 (8-ounce) cartons vanilla low-fat yogurt

1 cup halved seedless red grapes

1 medium banana, peeled and sliced

1 (8.25-ounce) can apricot halves in juice, drained and sliced

1 (8-ounce) can pineapple chunks in juice, drained

2 tablespoons no-sugar-added apricot spread

¼ cup flaked coconut, toasted

PER SERVING

190 Calories

36.7g Carbohydrate

3.1g Fat (2.4g saturated)

2.2g Fiber

3.7g Protein

3mg Cholesterol

57mg Sodium

110mg Calcium

0.6mg Iron

1. Spoon yogurt onto several layers of heavy-duty paper towels; spread to ½-inch thickness. Cover with additional paper towels; let stand 5 minutes.

2. While yogurt stands, combine grapes and next 3 ingredients in a bowl; spoon evenly into individual dessert dishes.

3. Scrape yogurt from paper towels into a small bowl, using a rubber spatula. Stir apricot spread into yogurt; spoon yogurt mixture evenly over fruit. Sprinkle with coconut. Yield: 4 (¾-cup) servings.

Serve with roasted turkey breast, glazed carrots, and steamed broccoli.

To toast the coconut, spread it in a thin layer in the bottom of a pieplate, and microwave at HIGH 1 to 2 minutes, stirring every 30 seconds.

Fresh Pears in Blackberry Wine Sauce

6   firm ripe Bosc pears, peeled and cored
1½   cups red wine or nonalcoholic red wine
¼   cup firmly packed brown sugar
1   tablespoon lemon juice
¼   teaspoon ground cinnamon
1   tablespoon cornstarch
1   tablespoon cold water
1   cup fresh or frozen blackberries, thawed

1. Cut each pear into 8 wedges; set aside.

2. Combine wine and next 3 ingredients in a large skillet; place over high heat, and bring to a boil. Reduce heat to low, and add pears to skillet. Cover and simmer 5 minutes or just until pears are tender. Using a slotted spoon, remove pears from wine mixture, and arrange 8 wedges on each of six individual dessert plates; set aside.

3. Combine cornstarch and water, stirring until smooth. Gradually add to wine mixture, stirring well. Increase heat to medium-high, and bring wine mixture to boil; cook, stirring constantly, 1 minute or until thickened and bubbly. Remove from heat; gently stir in blackberries. Spoon sauce evenly over pears. Yield: 6 servings.

Serve with grilled pork tenderloin, roasted potatoes, and steamed broccoli.

You can substitute Anjou or Red Barlett pears in this recipe, but Bosc pears tend to hold their shape especially well when they are poached.

EXCHANGES
3 Fruit

POINTS
2

PER SERVING
161 Calories
41.3g Carbohydrate
0.8g Fat (0.0g saturated)
6.4g Fiber
1.0g Protein
0mg Cholesterol
8mg Sodium
41mg Calcium
1.0mg Iron

Rum-Glazed Pineapple

EXCHANGES

2 Fruit

½ Fat

POINTS

3

PER SERVING

134 Calories

27.5g Carbohydrate

3.1g Fat (1.4g saturated)

0.5g Fiber

0.6g Protein

0mg Cholesterol

35mg Sodium

28mg Calcium

0.7mg Iron

1 (20-ounce) can chunk pineapple in juice, undrained

2 teaspoons margarine

3 tablespoons brown sugar

2 tablespoons dark rum

¼ teaspoon cornstarch

2 tablespoons flaked coconut, toasted

1. Drain pineapple, reserving ⅓ cup juice.

2. Melt margarine in a large nonstick skillet over medium-high heat. Add pineapple juice, brown sugar, and pineapple chunks, stirring well. Bring to a boil; reduce heat, and simmer 2 to 3 minutes, stirring often.

3. Combine rum and cornstarch, stirring well; add to skillet. Cook 1 minute or until slightly thickened.

4. Spoon pineapple mixture into serving dish; sprinkle with coconut. Serve warm. Yield: 4 (½-cup) servings.

Serve with lemon-baked fish, rice, and steamed asparagus.

This recipe is easily doubled and saucy enough to serve over angel food cake. Instructions for toasting ¼ cup coconut are in the tip box on page 26. Keep the extra 2 tablespoons in the freezer to sprinkle over desserts or fruit salads.

Lemon Sorbet with Tropical Fruit Sauce

1   (11-ounce) can mandarin oranges in light syrup, undrained

1   teaspoon cornstarch

2   kiwifruit, peeled and sliced

3   cups lemon fat-free sorbet or nonfat ice cream

EXCHANGES

3 Fruit

POINTS

4

PER SERVING

191 Calories

47.9g Carbohydrate

0.2g Fat (0.0g saturated)

0.9g Fiber

0.4g Protein

0mg Cholesterol

3mg Sodium

7mg Calcium

0.2mg Iron

1. Drain oranges, reserving juice; set oranges aside.

2. Combine juice and cornstarch in a small saucepan over medium-high heat. Bring to a boil; reduce heat to medium and cook 1 minute, or until thickened. Place saucepan in bowl of ice; let stand 5 minutes or until cool, stirring often. Stir in oranges and kiwifruit.

3. Spoon ½ cup sorbet into individual dessert bowls. Spoon fruit sauce evenly over sorbet. Yield: 6 servings.

Serve with barbecued chicken and steamed summer squash.

Kiwifruit tastes like a blend of strawberry and banana. If you can't find kiwifruit, instead use 1 small banana, sliced, and 6 sliced fresh strawberries.

Chocolate-Almond Fondue

1   (14-ounce) can fat-free sweetened condensed milk

½   cup reduced-fat semisweet chocolate baking chips

½   teaspoon almond extract

24   fresh strawberries

24   (1-inch) cubes angel food cake (about ¼ of 16-ounce cake)

1. Combine milk and chocolate in a medium saucepan over low heat. Cook, stirring constantly, about 3 minutes or until chocolate melts. Remove from heat, and stir in almond extract. Serve warm with strawberries and cake. Yield: 24 servings (1 tablespoon sauce, 1 strawberry, and 1 cake cube per serving).

Serve with turkey chili, green salad, and breadsticks.

> To serve a traditional fondue dessert, keep the sauce warm in a fondue pot or chafing dish. Let guests dip strawberries and cake into the warm sauce with fondue sticks or wooden picks. Or, use the sauce to top ice cream or to drizzle over cake or fruit. The recipe makes 1½ cups of sauce.

Peach Melba Brûlée (photo, page 21)

1	(29-ounce) can sliced peaches in extra-light syrup, undrained
3	ounces angel food cake, cut into ½-inch cubes (about 2 cups)
¼	cup no-sugar-added seedless raspberry spread
¾	cup low-fat sour cream
¼	cup plus 2 tablespoons brown sugar

1. Drain peaches, reserving 1 tablespoon syrup; pat peaches dry with paper towels. Set aside.

2. Divide cake cubes evenly into 6 (8-ounce) ramekins or custard cups. Combine raspberry spread and reserved peach syrup; stir until smooth. Spoon 2 teaspoons raspberry mixture over cake in each dish. Spoon peaches evenly over raspberry mixture; top each serving with 2 tablespoons sour cream. Sprinkle each with 1 tablespoon brown sugar.

3. Place ramekins on a baking sheet. Broil 5½ inches from heat (with electric oven door partially opened) 3 minutes or until sugar melts and begins to bubble. Serve immediately. Yield: 6 servings.

Serve with lemon chicken, rice, and steamed asparagus.

A brûlée (French for "burned") is a dessert featuring sugar that has been caramelized at high heat. If you don't have dishes that are safe for the broiler, bake the brûlé at 400° for 10 minutes for a "melted" sugar dessert.

EXCHANGES
1 Starch
2 Fruit
1 Fat

POINTS
4

PER SERVING
205 Calories
42.2g Carbohydrate
3.6g Fat (2.2g saturated)
0.8g Fiber
1.7g Protein
11mg Cholesterol
98mg Sodium
55mg Calcium
0.3mg Iron

Peach Shortcakes

EXCHANGES
1 Starch
2 Fruit
1 Fat

POINTS
5

PER SERVING
240 Calories
44.6g Carbohydrate
5.2g Fat (1.1g saturated)
1.3g Fiber
3.8g Protein
1mg Cholesterol
434mg Sodium
31mg Calcium
0.1mg Iron

Remove the lid, and thaw a 4-ounce carton of whipped topping in the microwave at MEDIUM-LOW (30% power) for 1 to 2 minutes.

1	cup plus 2 tablespoons low-fat biscuit and baking mix
3	tablespoons sugar, divided
⅛	teaspoon ground cinnamon
⅛	teaspoon ground nutmeg
⅓	cup low-fat milk
1	tablespoon margarine, melted
2	cups frozen sliced peaches
¼	cup frozen fat-free whipped topping, thawed

1. Combine biscuit mix, 2 tablespoons sugar, cinnamon, and nutmeg; stir well. Add milk and margarine, stirring just until combined.

2. Drop dough by spoonfuls onto an ungreased baking sheet, spreading each mound to a 3-inch circle. Bake at 425° for 7 minutes or until golden.

3. While shortcakes bake, place peaches in a microwave-safe bowl. Microwave at MEDIUM-LOW (30% power) 5 to 6 minutes or until thawed. Use a fork to break apart peaches. Sprinkle peaches with remaining 1 tablespoon sugar; stir well.

4. Split each shortcake in half horizontally. Place bottom halves of cakes on individual dessert plates. Top each with ½ cup peach mixture. Arrange remaining cake halves over peaches. Top each with 1 tablespoon whipped topping. Serve warm. Yield: 4 servings.

Serve with oven-baked chicken, mashed potatoes, and steamed green beans.

Orange-Strawberry Trifle

3   (8-ounce) cartons orange cream low-fat yogurt
1   (8-ounce) carton nonfat sour cream
2   (11-ounce) cans mandarin oranges in light syrup, undrained
1   tablespoon Grand Marnier or other orange-flavored liqueur
8   ounces angel food cake, cut into ¾-inch cubes (about 5 cups)
4   cups fresh strawberries, halved
Mint sprig (optional)

1. Combine yogurt and sour cream; set aside.

2. Drain oranges, reserving 3 tablespoons syrup. Set aside oranges. Combine syrup and liqueur.

3. Arrange half of cake cubes in a 2-quart trifle bowl. Pour half of syrup mixture evenly over cake cubes. Top with half of yogurt mixture. Arrange half of oranges and strawberries over yogurt. Repeat procedure with remaining cake, syrup mixture, yogurt mixture, and fruit. Serve immediately or chill up to 3 hours. Just before serving, garnish with mint, if desired. Yield: 8 servings.

Serve with grilled shrimp, couscous, and grilled vegetable kabobs.

Substitute mandarin orange syrup from the can or orange juice for Grand Marnier, if desired.

EXCHANGES
2½ Starch
1 Fruit

POINTS
4

PER SERVING
237 Calories
48.8g Carbohydrate
1.1g Fat (0.4g saturated)
1.7g Fiber
7.5g Protein
8mg Cholesterol
215mg Sodium
33mg Calcium
0.4mg Iron

Chocolate-Glazed Coconut Cream Cake

EXCHANGES

2½ Starch

POINTS

4

PER SERVING

184 Calories

37.7g Carbohydrate

1.6g Fat (1.3g saturated)

0.0g Fiber

3.1g Protein

2mg Cholesterol

287mg Sodium

54mg Calcium

0.0mg Iron

1   (3.4-ounce) package coconut cream instant pudding mix

1¾ cups fat-free milk

¼   cup canned reduced-fat milk chocolate-flavored frosting (such as
     Sweet Rewards)

2   teaspoons fat-free milk

1   (13.6-ounce) fat-free pound cake

1. Prepare pudding mix according to package directions, using 1¾ cups milk. Cover and chill 5 minutes.

2. Combine frosting and milk in a small bowl, stirring well. Set aside.

3. Using a sharp serrated or an electric knife, slice cake horizontally into 4 layers. Spoon ⅓ cup pudding on bottom layer. Top with a layer of cake. Repeat procedure twice, ending with top cake layer. (Reserve remaining pudding for another use.) Pour glaze over cake. Slice with a sharp serrated knife or an electric knife. Yield: 10 servings.

Serve with pork loin chops, glazed carrots, and green beans.

For a warm glaze heat the frosting and milk mixture in the microwave at HIGH for 20 seconds.

Lemon-Raspberry Tarts (photo, page 40)

1 tablespoon plus 1 teaspoon no-sugar-added raspberry spread
1 (2.1-ounce) package frozen miniature phyllo shells
¼ cup plus 1 tablespoon lemon curd
½ cup frozen fat-free whipped topping, thawed
15 fresh raspberries
Mint sprigs (optional)

1. Spoon ¼ teaspoon raspberry spread into the bottom of each frozen phyllo shell. Spoon 1 teaspoon lemon curd over raspberry spread in each shell. Spoon whipped topping evenly over lemon curd.

2. Place 1 raspberry on each tart. Garnish with mint, if desired. Yield: 15 tarts.

Serve with chicken salad, fresh tomato slices, and crisp breadsticks.

You can make these tarts at least 3 hours ahead and store them in the refrigerator. You don't need to thaw the phyllo shells before filling them.

EXCHANGES
½ Starch

POINTS
1

PER SERVING
48 Calories
8.0g Carbohydrate
0.1g Fat (0.0g saturated)
0.2g Fiber
0.5g Protein
0mg Cholesterol
11mg Sodium
1mg Calcium
0.0mg Iron

Caramel-Toffee Parfaits

EXCHANGES

2 Starch

1 Fruit

½ Fat

POINTS

5

PER SERVING

226 Calories

48.9g Carbohydrate

2.2g Fat (1.3g saturated)

0.9g Fiber

4.1g Protein

0mg Cholesterol

109mg Sodium

2mg Calcium

0.1mg Iron

1	large banana, peeled
2	cups vanilla nonfat ice cream
2	tablespoons plus 2 teaspoons fat-free caramel or chocolate topping
1	(1.4-ounce) chocolate toffee crisp bar, finely crushed

1. Cut banana in half crosswise. Cut each banana half in half length-wise. Place 1 banana piece in each of four (4-ounce) parfait glasses.

2. Spoon ¼ cup ice cream into bottom of each parfait glass; top each with 1 teaspoon caramel topping. Sprinkle half of crushed candy evenly over parfaits. Repeat layers. Serve immediately. Yield: 4 servings.

Serve with chicken fajitas and black beans.

> For a no-mess way to crush the candy bar, place it in a zip-top plastic bag, seal the bag, and crush it with a rolling pin.

Chocolate-Peppermint Parfaits (photo, page 40)

⅓ cup finely crushed hard peppermint candies (about 11 candies),
divided
2¼ cups frozen fat-free whipped topping, thawed
1 (3.9-ounce) package instant chocolate fudge pudding mix
1¾ cups fat-free milk

1. Set aside 1 tablespoon crushed candies. Fold remaining crushed candies into whipped topping; set aside ½ cup plus 2 tablespoons topping mixture. Spoon remaining whipped topping mixture evenly into five parfait glasses.

2. Prepare pudding mix according to package directions, using fat-free milk. Layer half of pudding evenly over topping mixture in glasses. Repeat layers.

3. Top each parfait with 2 tablespoons reserved topping mixture; sprinkle evenly with reserved tablespoon crushed candies. Yield: 5 servings.

Serve with turkey burgers and roasted potatoes.

To crush the peppermints, place the candies in a heavy-duty, zip-top plastic bag. Seal and crush the candy by pounding it with a meat mallet or a heavy rolling pin.

EXCHANGES
3 Starch

POINTS
4

PER SERVING
212 Calories
47.8g Carbohydrate
0.1g Fat (0.1g saturated)
0.8g Fiber
3.7g Protein
2mg Cholesterol
375mg Sodium
105mg Calcium
0.0mg Iron

10 minutes

Cocoa-Cranberry Crispy Bars

EXCHANGES

½ Starch

1 Fruit

½ Fat

POINTS

3

PER SERVING

121 Calories

24.4g Carbohydrate

2.8g Fat (1.2g saturated)

0.3g Fiber

0.9g Protein

0mg Cholesterol

86mg Sodium

2mg Calcium

0.1mg Iron

1   (10-ounce) package large marshmallows

2   tablespoons margarine

6   cups chocolate-flavored crisp rice cereal

1   cup sweetened dried cranberries or raisins

½   cup miniature semisweet chocolate morsels

Vegetable cooking spray

1. Combine marshmallows and margarine in a large microwave-safe bowl. Microwave at HIGH 2 minutes. Stir well, and microwave 1 additional minute.

2. Meanwhile, combine cereal, cranberries, and chocolate morsels in a large bowl. Pour marshmallow mixture over cereal mixture, stirring until well combined.

3. Press cereal mixture into a 13- x 9- x 2-inch baking dish coated with cooking spray. Let cool completely; cut into bars. Yield: 24 bars.

Serve with fat-free milk as a snack.

Coat the spoon with cooking spray before you stir the cereal into the marshmallow mixture; this will keep the cereal from sticking to the spoon.

Banana-Berry
Smoothie
(recipe, page 42)

Chocolate-
Peppermint Parfaits
(recipe, page 37)

Lemon-Raspberry Tarts
(recipe, page 35)

40

Frosty Coffee Shake

½ cup fat-free milk

1 to 2 teaspoons instant coffee granules

1 cup vanilla nonfat ice cream

½ teaspoon vanilla extract

1 cup crushed ice

1. Combine milk and coffee granules, stirring until coffee dissolves.

2. Place ice cream in container of an electric blender; add milk mixture and vanilla. Cover and process until smooth, stopping once to scrape down sides. Add enough ice to bring mixture to 2-cup level. Cover and process until smooth. Serve immediately. Yield: 2 (1-cup) servings.

Serve with fresh strawberries as a snack.

Substitute nonfat chocolate ice cream for vanilla to make a mocha shake.

EXCHANGES
2 Starch

POINTS
3

PER SERVING
128 Calories

26.6g Carbohydrate

0.1g Fat (0.1g saturated)

0.0g Fiber

5.2g Protein

1mg Cholesterol

78mg Sodium

77mg Calcium

0.1mg Iron

Banana-Berry Smoothie (photo, page 39)

EXCHANGES
2 Starch
1 Fruit

POINTS
4

PER SERVING
202 Calories
47.9g Carbohydrate
0.4g Fat (0.2g saturated)
2.7g Fiber
5.1g Protein
1mg Cholesterol
63mg Sodium
54mg Calcium
0.8mg Iron

1   cup frozen unsweetened strawberries
1   small banana (about 5 ounces)
¼   cup fat-free milk
1   cup vanilla nonfat ice cream
Banana slices (optional)

1. Combine first 3 ingredients in container of an electric blender; cover and process until smooth, stopping once to scrape down sides. Add ice cream; blend until smooth. Garnish with banana slices, if desired. Yield: 2 (1-cup) servings.

Serve as a dessert beverage with spaghetti and a tossed green salad.

Serve this thick and creamy dessert with a spoon. For an extra-special touch (and 50 calories) place a Viennese wafer in each glass. Look for cans or boxes of the thin, rolled cookies on the specialty food aisle.

fish & shellfish

Baked Catfish in Foil Packets

EXCHANGES

3 Lean Meat

POINTS

3

PER SERVING

151 Calories

1.9g Carbohydrate

6.1g Fat (1.3g saturated)

0.4g Fiber

21.1g Protein

66mg Cholesterol

223mg Sodium

51mg Calcium

1.5mg Iron

1	tablespoon reduced-sodium soy sauce
1	teaspoon ground ginger
1	teaspoon sesame oil
4	(4-ounce) catfish fillets
¼	cup sliced green onions (about 2 large)
½	cup chopped sweet red pepper (about ½ medium)
½	cup peeled, finely chopped cucumber (about ½ small)

1. Combine soy sauce, ginger, and oil, stirring well.

2. Tear off four 12-inch squares of aluminum foil; place a fish fillet in center of each square. Spoon green onions, sweet pepper, and cucumber evenly over each fillet. Spoon soy sauce mixture evenly over vegetables. Fold foil over fillets to make packets, and seal edges tightly.

3. Place fish packets on a baking sheet; bake at 450° for 12 minutes. Yield: 4 servings.

Serve with a tossed green salad and garlic bread.

> You can substitute flounder, orange roughy, sole, perch, or grouper for catfish in this recipe.

Flounder in Orange Sauce

⅓ cup low-sugar orange marmalade
2 tablespoons unsweetened orange juice
¼ teaspoon ground ginger
⅓ cup sliced green onions (about 3 medium)
4 (4-ounce) flounder fillets (or orange roughy, cod, or perch)
Vegetable cooking spray

1. Combine first 3 ingredients in a small saucepan. Cook over medium heat until marmalade melts, stirring often. Remove from heat, and stir in green onions.

2. Place fillets in a 13- x 9- x 2-inch baking dish coated with cooking spray. Spoon orange marmalade mixture evenly over fillets. Bake at 400° for 10 minutes or until fish flakes easily when tested with a fork. Yield: 4 servings.

Serve with rice and steamed asparagus.

Slice green onions easily with kitchen scissors. Just hold a bunch of onions together and snip them over a measuring cup to save cleanup.

EXCHANGES
3 Very Lean Meat

POINTS
2

PER SERVING
117 Calories
2.9g Carbohydrate
1.5g Fat (0.3g saturated)
0.3g Fiber
21.8g Protein
54mg Cholesterol
98mg Sodium
39mg Calcium
0.6mg Iron

Flounder with Pimiento (photo, page 59)

EXCHANGES
3 Very Lean Meat

POINTS
2

PER SERVING
108 Calories
1.6g Carbohydrate
1.5g Fat (0.3g saturated)
0.0g Fiber
21.5g Protein
54mg Cholesterol
93mg Sodium
21mg Calcium
0.6mg Iron

Substitute 2 tablespoons of lemon juice for fresh juice from 1 small lemon.

1   small lemon
1   (2-ounce) jar diced pimiento, drained
4   (4-ounce) flounder fillets (or orange roughy, cod, or perch)
Butter-flavored vegetable cooking spray
1   teaspoon extra-spicy salt-free herb-and-spice blend (Mrs. Dash)
Fresh oregano sprigs (optional)

1. Cut lemon in half. Squeeze juice from half of lemon (about 1 table-spoon) into a small bowl; set remaining lemon half aside. Add pimiento to lemon juice, mixing well.

2. Place flounder in an 11- x 7- x 1½-inch baking dish coated with cooking spray. Coat fish with cooking spray; sprinkle with herb-and-spice blend.

3. Spoon pimiento mixture evenly over fish. Bake, uncovered, at 425° for 12 minutes or until fish flakes easily when tested with a fork. While fish bakes, cut remaining lemon half into slices to serve with fish. Garnish with oregano sprigs, if desired. Yield: 4 servings.

Serve with angel hair pasta, steamed snow peas, and dinner rolls.

Grilled Grouper with Tomato Salsa

1   medium tomato, seeded and chopped (about 1 cup)
3   tablespoons finely chopped purple onion
2   tablespoons chopped fresh cilantro or parsley
1   tablespoon lime juice
4   (4-ounce) grouper fillets (or red snapper or halibut)
⅛   teaspoon salt
Olive oil-flavored vegetable cooking spray

1. Combine first 4 ingredients, tossing gently; set aside.

2. Sprinkle both sides of fillets with salt. Arrange fillets in a grill basket coated with cooking spray; place basket on grill rack over medium-hot coals (350° to 400°). Grill, covered, 8 minutes or until fish flakes easily when tested with a fork, turning basket once.

3. Arrange fillets evenly on four individual serving plates. Top each serving with ¼ cup salsa. Yield: 4 servings.

Serve with roasted green and sweet red pepper strips and garlic bread.

Seeding the tomato keeps the salsa from being watery. To seed the tomato, cut it in half horizontally, and scoop out the seeds with a spoon.

EXCHANGES
3 Very Lean Meat
1 Vegetable

POINTS
2

PER SERVING
125 Calories
4.4g Carbohydrate
1.5g Fat (0.3g saturated)
1.1g Fiber
22.7g Protein
42mg Cholesterol
127mg Sodium
27mg Calcium
1.4mg Iron

Oriental Grouper

EXCHANGES

3 Very Lean Meat

POINTS

3

PER SERVING

131 Calories

5.1g Carbohydrate

1.3g Fat (0.3g saturated)

0.1g Fiber

23.3g Protein

42mg Cholesterol

854mg Sodium

39mg Calcium

1.6mg Iron

Garlic-flavored vegetable cooking spray

4   (4-ounce) grouper fillets (or red snapper or halibut)

⅓   cup reduced-sodium soy sauce

⅓   cup dry sherry

2   teaspoons sugar

¼   cup sliced green onions (about 2 large)

1. Place a large nonstick skillet coated with cooking spray over medium-high heat until hot. Add fillets, and cook 4 minutes on each side; remove fillets from skillet, and keep warm.

2. Combine soy sauce, sherry, and sugar; add mixture to hot skillet. Cook over high heat 3 minutes or until mixture thickens, stirring constantly to loosen particles that cling to bottom of skillet.

3. Return fillets to skillet, turning to coat with glaze. Transfer fillets to individual serving plates; sprinkle green onions evenly over fish, and serve immediately. Yield: 4 servings.

Serve with rice and steamed baby carrots.

It's fine to substitute ⅓ cup of white wine for the sherry; the flavor just won't be quite as sweet.

Grouper with Honey Citrus Glaze (photo, page 1)

3   tablespoons orange juice concentrate, thawed
2   tablespoons honey
1   teaspoon dried basil
¼   teaspoon garlic powder
6   dashes of hot sauce
4   (4-ounce) grouper fillets (or red snapper or halibut)
Vegetable cooking spray
Orange rind strips (optional)

1. Combine first 5 ingredients, stirring well.

2. Arrange fillets in a single layer in a grill basket coated with cooking spray. Grill, covered, over medium-hot coals (350° to 400°) for 5 minutes on each side or until fish flakes easily when tested with a fork, basting occasionally with orange juice mixture. Transfer fillets to a serving platter. Garnish with orange rind, if desired. Yield: 4 servings.

Serve with steamed asparagus and French bread slices.

To broil instead of grill, place the fish on the rack of a broiler pan coated with cooking spray. Broil 5½ inches from heat (with the electric oven door partially opened) for 5 minutes on each side. Baste the fish occasionally with the orange juice mixture.

EXCHANGES
3 Very Lean Meat

POINTS
3

PER SERVING
161 Calories
14.1g Carbohydrate
1.4g Fat (0.3g saturated)
0.2g Fiber
22.4g Protein
42mg Cholesterol
50mg Sodium
29mg Calcium
1.2mg Iron

Dijon Fish Fillets

EXCHANGES

3 Very Lean Meat

POINTS

2

PER SERVING

115 Calories

5.5g Carbohydrate

1.8g Fat (0.1g saturated)

0.0g Fiber

17.5g Protein

23mg Cholesterol

463mg Sodium

6mg Calcium

0.4mg Iron

1   (8-ounce) orange roughy fillet (or flounder, perch, or sole)

Butter-flavored vegetable cooking spray

1   tablespoon Dijon mustard

1½   teaspoons lemon juice

1   teaspoon reduced-sodium Worcestershire sauce

2   tablespoons Italian-seasoned breadcrumbs

1. Arrange fillet in an 11- x 7- x 1½-inch baking dish coated with cooking spray. Combine mustard, lemon juice, and Worcestershire sauce, stirring well; spread mixture evenly over fillet. Sprinkle breadcrumbs evenly over fish.

2. Bake, uncovered, at 450° for 12 minutes or until fish flakes easily when tested with a fork. Cut fillet in half, and serve immediately. Yield: 2 servings.

Serve with couscous and steamed broccoli.

Dijon mustard has a strong, distinctive flavor. For a flavor variation, use honey mustard, sweet-hot mustard, or spicy mustard.

Wine-Baked Orange Roughy

4   (4-ounce) orange roughy fillets (or flounder or sole)
Vegetable cooking spray
¼   teaspoon salt
¼   teaspoon ground pepper
⅛   teaspoon garlic powder
¼   cup sliced green onions (about 2 large)
1   (2-ounce) jar diced pimiento, drained
¼   cup lemon juice
¼   cup dry white wine

1. Place fillets in an 11- x 7- x 1½-inch baking dish coated with cooking spray; sprinkle fillets evenly with salt, pepper, garlic powder, green onions, and pimiento. Pour lemon juice and wine over fish.

2. Cover and bake at 400° for 10 minutes or until fish flakes easily when tested with a fork. Serve with a slotted spatula. Yield: 4 servings.

Serve with a spinach salad and French baguette slices.

To determine if fish is done, prick the thickest part with a fork. The fish will fall apart in flakes and the juices will be milky white if the fish is done.

EXCHANGES
3 Very Lean Meat

POINTS
2

PER SERVING
102 Calories
3.3g Carbohydrate
1.1g Fat (0.0g saturated)
0.2g Fiber
17.2g Protein
23mg Cholesterol
223mg Sodium
9mg Calcium
0.8mg Iron

Seaside Stir-Fry (photo, page 59)

EXCHANGES

2 Very Lean Meat

2 Starch

1 Vegetable

POINTS

5

PER SERVING

260 Calories

34.9g Carbohydrate

3.7g Fat (0.4g saturated)

2.6g Fiber

20.8g Protein

23mg Cholesterol

813mg Sodium

35mg Calcium

2.4mg Iron

Vegetable cooking spray

1   teaspoon sesame oil

3   tablespoons reduced-sodium soy sauce

1   teaspoon cornstarch

½   teaspoon ground ginger

¼   teaspoon garlic powder

3   green onions, cut into 2-inch pieces

1   medium carrot, scraped and sliced

½   medium-size sweet red pepper, cut into thin strips

8   ounces orange roughy (flounder, or sole fillets), cut into bite-size pieces

1   cup hot cooked rice

1. Coat a wok or medium-size nonstick skillet with cooking spray; add oil. Place over medium-high heat until hot. While wok heats, combine soy sauce, cornstarch, ginger, and garlic powder, stirring well; set aside.

2. Add vegetables to hot wok, and stir-fry 3 minutes or until crisp-tender. Add fish, and stir-fry 1 minute. Stir soy sauce mixture; add to wok. Reduce heat to medium-low, and cook 2 minutes, tossing often or until soy sauce mixture is slightly thickened and fish flakes easily when tested with a fork. Serve immediately over hot cooked rice. Yield: 2 servings.

Serve with sesame bread sticks.

Put a regular size bag of quick-cooking rice on to cook before you start preparing this recipe. It will be done in 10 minutes and yield 2 cups of cooked rice. Refrigerate or freeze the extra cup of rice; it reheats well in the microwave.

Salmon with Cucumber-Dill Sauce

1   cup dry white wine

½   cup water

1   tablespoon lemon juice

4   (4-ounce) salmon steaks (½ inch thick) or 1 (16-ounce) salmon fillet

¾   cup nonfat yogurt

½   cup unpeeled finely chopped cucumber (about ½ small)

1   teaspoon dried dillweed or 1 tablespoon chopped fresh dillweed

¼   teaspoon salt

1. Combine first 3 ingredients in a large nonstick skillet; stir well. Bring mixture to a boil over medium heat. Reduce heat to low, and add salmon steaks to skillet. Simmer 8 minutes or until fish flakes easily when tested with a fork.

2. While salmon cooks, combine yogurt, cucumber, dillweed, and salt; stir well.

3. Gently transfer salmon to a serving platter, using two spatulas; spoon cucumber sauce evenly over each steak. Yield: 4 servings.

Serve with herbed new potatoes and steamed asparagus.

Salmon steaks come with the skin on. Cook and serve the salmon without removing the skin to help the steaks hold an attractive shape.

EXCHANGES

4 Lean Meat

POINTS

5

PER SERVING

219 Calories

4.3g Carbohydrate

9.8g Fat (1.8g saturated)

0.1g Fiber

26.8g Protein

78mg Cholesterol

239mg Sodium

99mg Calcium

0.7mg Iron

Salmon with Pineapple Salsa (photo, page 57)

(photo, page 57)

EXCHANGES

3 Lean Meat

1 Starch

POINTS

6

PER SERVING

255 Calories

15.2g Carbohydrate

10.0g Fat (1.7g saturated)

0.5g Fiber

24.7g Protein

77mg Cholesterol

181mg Sodium

19mg Calcium

1.1mg Iron

4   (4-ounce) salmon fillets (½ inch thick)

Vegetable cooking spray

1   tablespoon reduced-sodium soy sauce

1   (20-ounce) can pineapple tidbits in juice, drained

½   cup finely chopped green pepper (about ½ medium)

¼   cup finely chopped purple onion (about ½ small)

1   medium jalapeño pepper, seeded and minced

1   tablespoon fresh lime juice

1. Arrange fillets on rack of a broiler pan coated with cooking spray; brush fillets with soy sauce. Broil 5½ inches from heat (with electric oven door partially opened) for 4 minutes on each side.

2. While salmon broils, combine pineapple and remaining 4 ingredients in a small bowl.

3. Transfer salmon fillets to a serving platter; top evenly with salsa. Yield: 4 servings.

Serve with rice and roasted zucchini and yellow squash strips.

Use rubber or plastic gloves to protect your skin when handling jalapeños or other hot peppers. If you want to reduce the heat in the salsa, remove the seeds and inner white veins or membranes from the pepper.

Lemon-Dill Scallops and Snow Peas (photo, page 58)

Vegetable cooking spray

1   teaspoon reduced-calorie margarine

8   ounces bay scallops

6   ounces fresh snow pea pods, trimmed at stem end

⅛   teaspoon salt

¼   teaspoon dried dillweed or ¾ teaspoon chopped fresh dillweed

1½ teaspoons fresh lemon juice

1. Lightly coat a nonstick skillet with cooking spray; add margarine, and place over high heat until margarine melts. Add scallops; cook 2 minutes, stirring often. Add snow peas and remaining ingredients; cook 2 minutes, stirring often. Serve immediately. Yield: 2 servings.

Serve with a fresh fruit salad of strawberries, peaches, and pineapple.

When fresh snow peas aren't available, use frozen Sugar Snap peas instead.

EXCHANGES

3 Very Lean Meat

1 Vegetable

POINTS

3

PER SERVING

150 Calories

9.5g Carbohydrate

2.6g Fat (0.3g saturated)

2.2g Fiber

21.4g Protein

37mg Cholesterol

351mg Sodium

66mg Calcium

2.2mg Iron

Cold Sesame Shrimp and Pasta

EXCHANGES
2 Lean Meat
3 Starch

POINTS
7

PER SERVING
329 Calories
44.3g Carbohydrate
5.2g Fat (0.8g saturated)
2.1g Fiber
24.3g Protein
148mg Cholesterol
177mg Sodium
51mg Calcium
4.8mg Iron

8 ounces vermicelli, uncooked
1 pound peeled, deveined medium-size fresh shrimp (1¼ pounds unpeeled)
1½ teaspoons sesame oil
¼ cup seasoned rice vinegar
1 small cucumber, quartered lengthwise and sliced
½ cup diagonally sliced green onions (1-inch pieces) (about 4 large)
¼ teaspoon dried crushed red pepper
1 tablespoon chopped dry-roasted peanuts

1. Bring 2 quarts water to a boil in a large saucepan. Break pasta in half, add to boiling water, and cook 3 minutes. (Do not add salt or fat.)

2. Add shrimp to pasta, and cook 3 additional minutes or until shrimp turn pink. Drain pasta mixture; rinse under cold water until cool. Drain again. Transfer pasta and shrimp to a large bowl.

3. Add oil, vinegar, cucumber, green onions, and crushed pepper to pasta mixture; toss gently. Arrange pasta mixture evenly on four individual serving plates; sprinkle peanuts over each serving. Yield: 4 servings.

Serve with sliced fresh tomatoes and breadsticks.

Cooking the pasta and shrimp together in the same water saves time and cleanup, and it adds flavor to the pasta.

Salmon with Pineapple Salsa
(recipe, page 54)

Lemon-Dill Scallops
and Snow Peas
(recipe, page 55)

Flounder with Pimiento
(recipe, page 46)

Seaside Stir-Fry
(recipe, page 52)

Shrimp and
Spinach Pasta

Shrimp and Spinach Pasta (photo, left)

8 ounces vermicelli, uncooked

Vegetable cooking spray

1 teaspoon olive oil

1 teaspoon minced garlic (about 2 cloves)

12 ounces peeled, deveined medium-size fresh shrimp (1 pound unpeeled)

¼ teaspoon dried crushed red pepper

1 (10-ounce) bag prewashed spinach leaves

2 plum tomatoes, cut into eighths

2 tablespoons fresh lemon juice

¼ teaspoon salt

Lemon wedges (optional)

EXCHANGES

2 Very Lean Meat

3 Starch

1 Vegetable

POINTS

6

PER SERVING

337 Calories

48.0g Carbohydrate

4.0g Fat (0.6g saturated)

4.6g Fiber

26.9g Protein

129mg Cholesterol

336mg Sodium

128mg Calcium

6.3mg Iron

1. Cook pasta according to package directions, omitting salt and fat. Drain well, reserving 3 tablespoons cooking water.

2. While pasta cooks, lightly coat a large nonstick skillet with cooking spray; add oil. Place over medium-high heat until hot; add garlic, and cook 1 minute, stirring often. Add shrimp and red pepper; cook 2 minutes, stirring often. Add spinach, tomato, lemon juice, salt, and reserved pasta water; cover and cook 3 minutes or until spinach wilts and shrimp turn pink.

3. Combine pasta and shrimp mixture in a large bowl; toss gently. Serve with lemon wedges, if desired. Yield: 4 servings.

Serve with crusty French rolls.

It saves time to buy shrimp already peeled from the seafood store or supermarket.

Spicy Baked Shrimp

EXCHANGES

2 Very Lean Meat

½ Starch

POINTS

3

PER SERVING

121 Calories

6.1g Carbohydrate

2.8g Fat (0.4g saturated)

0.0g Fiber

17.5g Protein

129mg Cholesterol

208mg Sodium

46mg Calcium

2.2mg Iron

Olive oil-flavored vegetable cooking spray

2   tablespoons lemon juice

1   tablespoon honey

2   teaspoons dried parsley flakes

2   teaspoons salt-free Creole seasoning

1   teaspoon olive oil

2   teaspoons reduced-sodium soy sauce

12   ounces peeled, deveined large fresh shrimp (1 pound unpeeled)

1. Coat an 11- x 7- x 1½-inch baking dish with cooking spray. Add lemon juice and next 5 ingredients to dish, stirring well. Add shrimp; toss well to coat. Bake at 450° for 8 minutes or until shrimp turn pink, stirring occasionally. Yield: 4 servings.

Serve with corn on the cob and coleslaw.

Rinse a measuring spoon or cup with cold water or spray with vegetable cooking spray before measuring honey; the honey will slide out easily.

meatless main dishes

Vegetable-Cheese Pizza (photo, page 2)

EXCHANGES

1 High-Fat Meat
2 Starch
1 Vegetable

POINTS

5

PER SERVING

262 Calories
35.0g Carbohydrate
7.4g Fat (4.1g saturated)
2.1g Fiber
13.3g Protein
16mg Cholesterol
617mg Sodium
186mg Calcium
1.1mg Iron

Vegetable cooking spray
2   medium-size green peppers, cut into thin strips
1   small onion, thinly sliced (about 3 ounces)
1   (8-ounce) package sliced fresh mushrooms
1   cup pizza sauce
1   (12.5-ounce) sun-dried tomato-flavored flat bread
5   (1-ounce) slices provolone cheese

1. Coat a large nonstick skillet with cooking spray; place over medium-high heat until hot. Add peppers, onion, and mushrooms; cook 8 minutes or until tender, stirring often.

2. While vegetables cook, spread pizza sauce over flat bread. Place directly on middle oven rack, and bake at 425° for 5 minutes.

3. Top pizza with vegetable mixture. Arrange cheese over vegetables, and bake 2 additional minutes or until cheese melts. Yield: 6 servings.

Serve with fresh melon slices.

You can use any flavor of flat bread or focaccia, or even individual flat bread crusts for this recipe.

Potato-Topped Vegetable Casserole

Olive oil-flavored vegetable cooking spray

2   cups frozen mixed vegetables, thawed

1   (15-ounce) can dark red kidney beans, drained

1   cup fat-free garlic-and-herb-flavored pasta sauce

½   teaspoon fennel seeds, crushed

½   teaspoon salt, divided

¼   teaspoon ground pepper

2   cups fat-free milk

2   cups instant potato flakes

¼   teaspoon paprika

EXCHANGES

3 Starch

1 Vegetable

POINTS

4

PER SERVING

276 Calories

53.0g Carbohydrate

1.5g Fat (0.3g saturated)

9.8g Fiber

13.9g Protein

2mg Cholesterol

879mg Sodium

205mg Calcium

2.1mg Iron

1. Coat a large nonstick skillet with cooking spray; place over medium-high heat until hot. Add vegetables, and cook 5 minutes or until vegetables are tender, stirring often. Stir in kidney beans, pasta sauce, fennel seeds, ¼ teaspoon salt, and pepper; cook 2 minutes or until thoroughly heated. Spoon vegetable mixture into a 1½-quart casserole coated with cooking spray.

2. Add milk to a medium saucepan, and place over medium-high heat until hot. Remove from heat; stir in potato flakes and remaining ¼ teaspoon salt; stir well. Spoon potato mixture over vegetables; sprinkle with paprika. Broil 5½ inches from heat (with electric over door partially opened) 5 minutes or until lightly browned. Yield: 4 servings.

Serve with cornbread.

Thaw the vegetables quickly in the microwave on MEDIUM-LOW (30% power) for 2 minutes.

Primavera Stuffed Potatoes

EXCHANGES

4 Starch

1 Fat

POINTS

5

PER SERVING

319 Calories

58.4g Carbohydrate

4.2g Fat (2.0g saturated)

8.1g Fiber

12.5g Protein

6mg Cholesterol

813mg Sodium

35mg Calcium

3.0mg Iron

2	(8-ounce) baking potatoes
1	(9-ounce) package frozen vegetables in Alfredo sauce
¼	teaspoon ground pepper
½	cup finely chopped tomato
1	small green onion, sliced
¼	cup nonfat sour cream
2	tablespoons fat-free Italian dressing

1. Pierce potatoes several times with a fork; place on a paper towel in microwave. Microwave at HIGH 8 minutes; turn potatoes. Cut a small slit in frozen vegetable packet; place in microwave with potatoes. Microwave at HIGH 7 additional minutes or until potatoes are tender and vegetables are hot.

2. Combine cooked vegetables, pepper, and remaining 4 ingredients in a bowl; stir well. Cut potatoes in half lengthwise; fluff with a fork. Spoon vegetable mixture over potato. Yield: 2 servings.

Serve with orange wedges and blueberries.

Larger potatoes take longer to cook in the microwave. Instructions for oven-baked potatoes are on page 17 in Just the Basics chapter.

Oriental Black Beans

8   cups thinly sliced napa cabbage, divided
2   (15-ounce) cans black beans, drained
1¼   cups chopped sweet red pepper (about 1 large)
1   cup fresh bean sprouts
¼   cup plus 2 tablespoons light toasted sesame soy and ginger
         vinaigrette (Olde Cape Cod)

1. Combine 2 cups cabbage, beans, and remaining 3 ingredients in a bowl, tossing well.

2. Divide remaining cabbage evenly among four individual serving plates. Spoon bean mixture evenly over sliced cabbage. Yield: 4 servings.

Serve with baked pita chips.

> The mild flavor and crisp texture of napa or Chinese cabbage is especially good in this recipe. You can substitute angel hair slaw, which is shredded, prepackaged cabbage. It has a slightly stronger flavor.

EXCHANGES

2 Starch

2 Vegetable

1 Fat

POINTS

4

PER SERVING

249 Calories

39.0g Carbohydrate

5.8g Fat (0.2g saturated)

7.2g Fiber

13.4g Protein

0mg Cholesterol

631mg Sodium

162mg Calcium

4.2mg Iron

Rice and Bean Soft Tacos

EXCHANGES
4 Starch
1 Fat

POINTS
6

PER SERVING
354 Calories
58.7g Carbohydrate
5.8g Fat (1.9g saturated)
5.7g Fiber
15.3g Protein
8mg Cholesterol
399mg Sodium
93mg Calcium
3.8mg Iron

4   (10-inch) flour tortillas

Vegetable cooking spray

½   cup thinly sliced green pepper (about ½ small)

½   cup thinly sliced onion (about ½ medium)

1   cup cooked long-grain rice (cooked without salt and fat)

1   (15-ounce) can no-salt-added black beans, drained

⅓   cup mild salsa

½   teaspoon chili powder

⅛   teaspoon salt

½   cup nonfat sour cream

¼   cup (1 ounce) shredded Monterey Jack cheese with peppers

1. Wrap tortillas in aluminum foil. Bake at 350° for 10 minutes or until tortillas are warm.

2. While tortillas bake, coat a nonstick skillet with cooking spray. Place over medium-high heat until hot. Add pepper and onion; cook 4 minutes or until tender, stirring often.

3. Combine rice and next 4 ingredients. Divide mixture evenly among warm tortillas; roll up, and place tortillas, seam side down, on a serving platter. Top with sour cream and cheese. Yield: 4 servings.

Serve with kiwifruit slices and strawberries.

> Leftover rice works well in this recipe. Or use quick-cooking rice that cooks in just 10 minutes. Instructions for cooking rice are in Just the Basics chapter on page 15.

Spicy Rice with Tofu

1	(4.5-ounce) package long grain and wild rice mix (such as Lipton)
1½	cups small broccoli flowerets
10	ounces firm tofu, drained and cubed
1	teaspoon hot sauce

1. Cook rice mix according to package directions, omitting fat. Let stand 2 to 3 minutes.

2. While rice cooks, arrange broccoli in a steamer basket over boiling water. Cover and steam 2 to 3 minutes or until crisp-tender.

3. Add broccoli, tofu, and hot sauce to rice in saucepan; toss well. Serve immediately. Yield: 3 servings.

Serve with red grapes.

This mixture is good served in a pita pocket. Substitute any fresh vegetable like zucchini, sweet red pepper, or carrots for the broccoli.

EXCHANGES

1 Medium-Fat Meat
2 Starch
1 Vegetable

POINTS

4

PER SERVING

221 Calories
35.0g Carbohydrate
4.8g Fat (0.6g saturated)
3.2g Fiber
11.8g Protein
0mg Cholesterol
604mg Sodium
96mg Calcium
4.4mg Iron

Sweet-and-Sour Tofu Stir-Fry (photo, page 79)

EXCHANGES
3 Starch
1 Vegetable
1 Fat

POINTS
6

PER SERVING
309 Calories
50.8g Carbohydrate
6.4g Fat (0.9g saturated)
5.8g Fiber
12.6g Protein
0mg Cholesterol
654mg Sodium
111mg Calcium
6.1mg Iron

1   extra-large bag quick-cooking boil-in-bag rice
Vegetable cooking spray
1   teaspoon sesame oil
1   (12-ounce) package firm tofu, drained and cubed
1   (21-ounce) package frozen Sweet and Sour Stir-Fry, thawed
2   tablespoons reduced-sodium soy sauce

1. Cook rice according to package directions, omitting salt and fat.

2. While rice cooks, coat a wok or large skillet with cooking spray; add oil. Place over medium-high heat until hot. Add tofu, and cook 4 to 5 minutes or until tofu is lightly browned, stirring often. Remove tofu, and drain.

3. Add sauce from stir-fry mix to wok, and cook 1 minute. Add vegetables; cover and cook 5 minutes or until vegetables are tender. Stir in soy sauce. Add tofu, stirring gently. Serve over rice. Yield: 3 servings.

Serve with French bread.

Stir the tofu gently while it cooks to keep it from crumbling.

Herbed Polenta with Portobellos (photo, page 78)

Olive oil-flavored vegetable cooking spray
1 (16-ounce) package Italian herb or plain polenta
½ cup grated Asiago or fresh Parmesan cheese, divided
1 (6-ounce) package sliced portobello mushrooms
½ cup sliced onion (about ½ medium)
¼ cup red wine
¼ cup canned vegetable broth
¼ to ½ teaspoon dried rosemary, crushed

1. Coat a large skillet with cooking spray; place over high heat until hot. While skillet heats, cut polenta into 9 slices. Add polenta slices to skillet, and cook 4 minutes on each side or until lightly browned.

2. Remove skillet from heat, and transfer polenta slices to a warm serving platter. While polenta is hot, sprinkle slices with half of cheese. Cover and keep warm.

3. Wipe skillet with paper towels, and coat with cooking spray; place over medium-high heat until hot. Add mushrooms and onion, and cook 4 minutes or until onion is crisp-tender, stirring often. Add wine, broth, and rosemary. Cook over high heat 1 minute or until most of liquid evaporates.

4. Spoon mushroom mixture evenly over polenta slices; sprinkle with remaining cheese. Serve immediately. Yield: 3 servings.

Serve with a spinach salad and whole wheat rolls.

> Look for packages of polenta in the produce section of your supermarket. The package shape is similar to that of ground sausage.

EXCHANGES
1 Starch
2 Vegetable
1 Fat

POINTS
4

PER SERVING
200 Calories
27.1g Carbohydrate
5.7g Fat (3.3g saturated)
3.0g Fiber
9.6g Protein
17mg Cholesterol
350mg Sodium
7mg Calcium
0.1mg Iron

Chili Mac (photo, page 78)

EXCHANGES

1 Lean Meat

4 Starch

1 Vegetable

POINTS

6

PER SERVING

369 Calories

61.9g Carbohydrate

3.4g Fat (1.7g saturated)

8.6g Fiber

22.0g Protein

9mg Cholesterol

776mg Sodium

146mg Calcium

2.7mg Iron

1½ cups elbow macaroni, uncooked

1 (15-ounce) cans vegetarian chili with beans (such as Hormel)

1 (16-ounce) can dark red kidney beans, drained

½ teaspoon chili powder

¾ cup (3 ounces) reduced-fat sharp Cheddar cheese, shredded

½ cup nonfat sour cream

Additional chili powder (optional)

1. Cook macaroni according to package directions, omitting salt and fat. Drain well, and set aside.

2. Combine chili, kidney beans, and chili powder in a large nonstick skillet; add macaroni. Cook over medium heat 5 minutes or until hot, stirring often. Spoon into individual serving bowls; sprinkle with cheese, and top evenly with sour cream. Sprinkle additional chili powder over sour cream, if desired. Yield: 6 servings.

Serve with a tossed green salad and corn sticks.

If you're watching your sodium intake, check the ingredient label on the chili powder container. Some brands add more salt than others.

Mediterranean Pasta

1	(9-ounce) package fresh cheese-filled tortellini
1	(16-ounce) jar fat-free marinara sauce (about 2 cups)
1	(14-ounce) can quartered artichoke hearts, coarsely chopped
3	tablespoons chopped ripe olives
2	tablespoons grated Parmesan cheese
2	tablespoons fine, dry breadcrumbs
½	teaspoon dried Italian seasoning

1. Cook pasta according to package directions, omitting salt and fat; drain.

2. While pasta cooks, place marinara sauce in a small saucepan, and cook over medium heat 4 to 5 minutes or until thoroughly heated, stirring occasionally.

3. Combine tortellini, sauce, artichokes, and olives in a 1½-quart casserole dish. Combine cheese, breadcrumbs, and seasoning; sprinkle over pasta mixture. Broil 3 inches from heat (with electric oven door partially opened) for 2 minutes or until lightly browned. Yield: 5 servings.

Serve with a tossed green salad and breadsticks.

EXCHANGES
2 Starch

2 Vegetable

1 Fat

POINTS
5

PER SERVING
253 Calories

38.6g Carbohydrate

4.1g Fat (2.9g saturated)

1.5g Fiber

12.3g Protein

34mg Cholesterol

811mg Sodium

104mg Calcium

1.2mg Iron

Look for fresh pasta in the refrigerated section of the supermarket.

Mostaccioli with Red Pepper Sauce

EXCHANGES
3 Starch
1 Vegetable

POINTS
5

PER SERVING
262 Calories
50.3g Carbohydrate
2.3g Fat (0.9g saturated)
2.2g Fiber
10.1g Protein
3mg Cholesterol
269mg Sodium
80mg Calcium
2.8mg Iron

Substitute rigatoni or penne pasta for mostaccioli.

8   ounces mostaccioli, uncooked
2   cups sliced zucchini (about 2 medium)
1   clove garlic
1   (7.25-ounce) jar roasted red peppers, drained
1   tablespoon balsamic vinegar
¼   cup nonfat mayonnaise
3   tablespoons grated Parmesan cheese
Chopped fresh basil (optional)

1. Cook pasta according to package directions, omitting salt and fat. Add zucchini, and cook 2 additional minutes or until zucchini is tender.

2. While pasta and zucchini cook, position knife blade in food processor bowl; drop garlic though food chute with processor running. Process until garlic is finely chopped. Add peppers and vinegar to processor; process 1 minute, stopping once to scrape down sides. Add mayonnaise and cheese; process just until combined.

3. Drain pasta-zucchini mixture; transfer to a large bowl. Add red pepper sauce to pasta, and toss gently. Garnish with chopped fresh basil, if desired. Yield: 4 servings.

Serve with a tossed green salad.

Penne with White Beans

8	ounces penne pasta, uncooked
2	(15-ounce) cans cannellini beans, drained
1	(7.25-ounce) jar chopped roasted red peppers, drained
½	cup chopped fresh basil
¼	cup balsamic vinegar
1	tablespoon olive oil
½	teaspoon salt
½	teaspoon ground black pepper
⅓	cup crumbled basil-and-tomato-flavored feta cheese

1. Cook pasta according to package directions, omitting salt and fat. Drain and return pasta to saucepan.

2. Add beans and next 6 ingredients to saucepan; toss gently. Spoon mixture onto individual serving plates, and sprinkle evenly with feta. Serve immediately. Yield: 7 servings.

Serve with fresh tomato slices and garlic breadsticks.

Chop the basil while the pasta cooks. The chopping is faster when you arrange the leaves in a stack and chop with a sharp knife.

EXCHANGES

2 Starch

2 Vegetable

1½ Fat

POINTS

5

PER SERVING

273 Calories

37.6g Carbohydrate

7.5g Fat (3.4g saturated)

5.1g Fiber

12.1g Protein

15mg Cholesterol

723mg Sodium

29mg Calcium

2.8mg Iron

Pasta with Asparagus and Walnuts (photo, right)

EXCHANGES
3 Starch
1 Vegetable
2 Fat

POINTS
6

PER SERVING
306 Calories
49.0g Carbohydrate
7.9g Fat (1.1g saturated)
5.7g Fiber
12.2g Protein
0mg Cholesterol
674mg Sodium
29mg Calcium
1.3mg Iron

1   (4.7-ounce) package angel hair pasta with lemon and butter (Pasta Roni)
2   cups water
½   cup sun-dried tomatoes (packed without oil), coarsely chopped
¾   pound fresh asparagus spears
¼   cup chopped walnuts, toasted

1. Cook pasta according to package directions, using 2 cups water and omitting fat. Stir sun-dried tomatoes into water with pasta.

2. While pasta cooks, snap off tough ends of asparagus. Remove scales with a vegetable peeler, if desired. Cut asparagus into 1-inch pieces. Add asparagus to pasta the last 2 minutes of cooking time. Drain well.

3. Add walnuts to pasta mixture, and toss gently. Let stand 5 minutes before serving. Yield: 3 servings.

Serve with crusty French rolls.

Instructions for toasting nuts are on page 20 in Just the Basics chapter.

Herbed Polenta with
Portobellos
(recipe, page 71)

Chili Mac
(recipe, page 72)

78

Sweet-and-Sour
Tofu Stir-Fry
(recipe, page 70)

Couscous with Italian Vegetable Ragoût (photo, left)

4 cups thinly sliced small zucchini (about 4)

2 cups coarsely chopped onion (about 1 medium)

2 (14½-ounce) cans Italian stewed tomatoes, undrained

1 (15-ounce) can no-salt-added garbanzo beans, drained

1 teaspoon dried Italian seasoning

¼ teaspoon salt

¼ teaspoon ground pepper

7 cups cooked couscous, cooked without salt and fat

EXCHANGES

4 Starch

POINTS

5

PER SERVING

295 Calories

61.6g Carbohydrate

1.4g Fat (0.1g saturated)

5.9g Fiber

11.2g Protein

0mg Cholesterol

503mg Sodium

73mg Calcium

2.8mg Iron

1. Combine zucchini and next 6 ingredients in a large skillet. Bring to a boil; cover, reduce heat, and simmer 10 minutes, stirring occasionally. Uncover and simmer 5 minutes or until most of liquid evaporates.

2. Arrange 1 cup couscous on each of seven individual serving plates; top with vegetable mixture. Yield: 7 servings.

Serve with Italian bread slices.

One (10-ounce) package of couscous makes 5 cups of cooked couscous, so be sure to buy two packages for this recipe.

Open-Faced Eggwich

EXCHANGES

1 High-Fat Meat

2½ Starch

POINTS

7

PER SERVING

297 Calories

39.6g Carbohydrate

9.3g Fat (2.6g saturated)

0.7g Fiber

14.6g Protein

227mg Cholesterol

592mg Sodium

219mg Calcium

2.7mg Iron

Cheddar Cheese Sauce

4   eggs

2   English muffins, split

4   slices tomato

3   tablespoons honey mustard

1. Add water to a medium skillet to depth of 2 inches; bring to a boil. (While water comes to a boil, prepare Cheddar Cheese Sauce.) Reduce heat to low. Break eggs, one at a time, into a saucer; slip eggs, one at a time, into simmering water, holding saucer as close as possible to surface of water. Simmer 6 to 7 minutes or until internal temperature of egg reaches 160° (yolk will be solid).

2. While eggs simmer, place muffin halves and tomato slices on a baking sheet. Broil 4 inches from heat (with electric oven door partially opened) 4 minutes or until muffins are toasted and tomato slices are warm. Spread muffins with mustard; top each with a tomato slice. Remove eggs from water with a slotted spoon, and place over tomato slices; top with Cheddar Cheese Sauce. Yield: 4 servings.

Cheddar Cheese Sauce

½   cup low-fat milk

2   teaspoons all-purpose flour

¼   cup (1 ounce) shredded reduced-fat sharp Cheddar cheese

⅛   teaspoon salt

1. Combine milk and flour in a small saucepan. Cook over medium heat, stirring constantly, until thickened and bubbly. Add cheese and salt, stirring until cheese melts. Yield: ½ cup.

Serve with fresh apple wedges.

> Egg yolks are less likely to break if you crack the eggs over a saucer. To crack shells gently, tap each egg firmly with the sharp edge of a table knife.

meats

Teriyaki Flank Steak

EXCHANGES
3 Medium-Fat Meat
½ Starch

POINTS
6

PER SERVING
237 Calories
7.2g Carbohydrate
13.0g Fat (5.5g saturated)
0.0g Fiber
22.0g Protein
60mg Cholesterol
366mg Sodium
7mg Calcium
2.3mg Iron

1   (1-pound) lean flank steak (½ inch thick)
¼   cup honey
¼   cup reduced-sodium soy sauce
1   teaspoon ground ginger
1   teaspoon sesame oil
½   teaspoon minced garlic (1 clove)
¼   teaspoon salt
¼   teaspoon ground pepper
Vegetable cooking spray

1. Place flank steak in a large heavy-duty, zip-top plastic bag. Combine honey and next 6 ingredients; stir well. Pour marinade over steak; seal bag securely. Turn bag to coat steak.

2. While grill heats, remove steak from marinade, reserving marinade. Place marinade in a small saucepan; bring to a boil. Remove from heat, and set aside.

3. Coat grill rack with cooking spray; place on grill over medium-hot coals (350° to 400°). Place steak on rack; grill, covered, 5 to 6 minutes on each side or to desired degree of doneness, basting occasionally with marinade. Slice steak diagonally across grain into ¼-inch-thick slices. Yield: 4 servings.

Serve with brown rice and steamed snow peas.

> Use a sharp knife or an electric knife to slice the steak into very thin slices.

Sirloin Steak with Garlic Sauce (photo, page 100)

Vegetable cooking spray

1 pound well-trimmed boneless top sirloin steak (1 inch thick)

1 teaspoon dried thyme

¼ teaspoon salt

¼ teaspoon ground pepper

8 large garlic cloves, unpeeled

⅓ cup canned no-salt-added beef broth

1. Coat rack of a broiler pan with cooking spray. Sprinkle both sides of steak with thyme, salt, and pepper. Place steaks on rack; arrange garlic cloves around steak.

2. Broil steak and garlic 5½ inches from heat (with electric oven door partially opened) 5 to 6 minutes on each side or to desired degree of doneness. Transfer steak to cutting board; cover loosely with aluminum foil to keep warm.

3. Position knife blade in food processor bowl. Cut off bottom of each garlic clove, and squeeze out soft garlic into processor bowl; process until smooth. Add broth; process until combined. Transfer garlic sauce to a microwave-safe dish. Microwave at HIGH 40 seconds.

4. Slice steak diagonally across grain into thin slices; spoon garlic sauce over steak. Yield: 4 servings.

Serve with mashed potatoes and steamed broccoli.

EXCHANGES

4 Very Lean Meat

POINTS

4

PER SERVING

188 Calories

2.5g Carbohydrate

6.6g Fat (2.5g saturated)

0.2g Fiber

27.7g Protein

80mg Cholesterol

208mg Sodium

28mg Calcium

3.6mg Iron

Roast extra cloves of garlic and freeze them for later.

Gingered Beef Stir-Fry (photo, page 98)

EXCHANGES

3 Lean Meat

1 Starch

POINTS

5

PER SERVING

249 Calories

12.1g Carbohydrate

8.7g Fat (2.5g saturated)

3.7g Fiber

28.8g Protein

69mg Cholesterol

316mg Sodium

64mg Calcium

5.8mg Iron

½   cup canned no-salt-added beef broth

1   tablespoon reduced-sodium soy sauce

1   teaspoon cornstarch

1   teaspoon ground ginger

¼   to ½ teaspoon dried crushed red pepper

Vegetable cooking spray

1   teaspoon dark sesame oil

½   pound lean boneless sirloin steak, cut crosswise into
      ¼-inch-thick slices

1   (9-ounce) package frozen Sugar Snap peas

1. Combine first 5 ingredients; stir well.

2. Coat a wok or large nonstick skillet with cooking spray; drizzle oil around top of wok, coating sides. Heat at medium-high (375°) until hot. Add steak, and stir-fry 2 minutes or until lightly browned.

3. Add peas and broth mixture to wok; stir-fry 3 minutes or until thickened. Yield: 2 servings.

Serve with rice and steamed yellow squash.

You can substitute snow peas or zucchini strips for Sugar Snap peas.

Mexican Cubed Steaks

Vegetable cooking spray

1   teaspoon vegetable oil

4   (4-ounce) lean cubed sirloin steaks

1   (8-ounce) jar medium or hot picante sauce

2   tablespoons lime juice

¼   teaspoon ground pepper

¼   cup chopped fresh cilantro or parsley

1. Coat a large nonstick skillet with cooking spray; add oil. Place over medium-high heat until hot. Add steaks; cook 2 minutes on each side.

2. Combine picante sauce, lime juice, and pepper; pour over steaks. Cover, reduce heat, and simmer 10 minutes. Sprinkle with cilantro. Yield: 4 servings.

Serve with rice, black beans, and fresh pineapple wedges.

EXCHANGES

3 Lean Meat

1 Starch

POINTS

5

PER SERVING

225 Calories

12.1g Carbohydrate

7.0g Fat (2.3g saturated)

1.6g Fiber

27.9g Protein

69mg Cholesterol

929mg Sodium

11mg Calcium

3.2mg Iron

Cubed steak is simply a steak that has been rolled through a machine that punches holes in the meat to tenderize it. If you don't see cubed steaks prepackaged at the meat counter, ask the butcher to cube some steaks for you.

Peppered Filets with Mushroom Sauce (photo, page 99)

EXCHANGES

3½ Lean Meat

1 Vegetable

POINTS

5

PER SERVING

211 Calories

6.8g Carbohydrate

8.7g Fat (3.2g saturated)

1.9g Fiber

26.7g Protein

71mg Cholesterol

62mg Sodium

23mg Calcium

5.0mg Iron

Freshly ground pepper is more pungent and flavorful than the ground pepper in cans or jars.

2   (4-ounce) beef tenderloin steaks (1 inch thick)
1   teaspoon freshly ground pepper
Vegetable cooking spray
1   (8-ounce) package sliced fresh mushrooms
2   green onions, sliced
¼   cup dry red wine or canned no-salt-added beef broth

1. Sprinkle both sides of steaks evenly with pepper.

2. Coat rack of a broiler pan with cooking spray. Place steaks on rack; broil 5½ inches from heat (with electric oven door partially opened) 5 to 6 minutes on each side or to desired degree of doneness.

3. While steaks broil, coat a large nonstick skillet with cooking spray; place over medium-high heat until hot. Add mushrooms and onions; cook 5 minutes or until mushrooms are tender. Add wine; simmer 1 minute.

4. Place steaks on a serving platter; spoon mushroom mixture over steaks. Yield: 2 servings.

Serve with garlic mashed potatoes and a tossed green salad.

Beef Patties with Sweet-and-Sour Onions

1	pound lean ground round
¼	teaspoon garlic powder
¼	teaspoon ground pepper

Olive oil–flavored vegetable cooking spray

1	(12-ounce) package frozen chopped onion (about 2½ cups)
2	tablespoons sugar
2	tablespoons balsamic vinegar

EXCHANGES
3 Lean Meat
1 Starch

POINTS
5

PER SERVING
226 Calories
15.6g Carbohydrate
5.9g Fat (2.1g saturated)
2.0g Fiber
26.3g Protein
66mg Cholesterol
68mg Sodium
27mg Calcium
2.7mg Iron

1. Combine first 3 ingredients; stir well. Shape meat mixture into 4 equal patties, ¼-inch-thick.

2. Coat a large nonstick skillet with cooking spray; place over medium-high heat until hot. Place patties in skillet, and cook 5 minutes on each side or until done.

3. While patties cook, thaw onion by placing in a strainer or colander under warm running water. Drain well. Transfer patties to a serving platter, and keep warm. Add onion, sugar, and vinegar to skillet; cook 4 minutes over medium heat or until onion mixture is slightly thickened. Pour onion mixture over patties, and serve immediately. Yield: 4 servings.

Serve with rice, steamed green peppers and sweet red peppers, and soft dinner rolls.

It's important to thaw the frozen onion and then drain well so the saucy gravy won't be watered down and thin.

Peppery Mushroom Burgers (photo, page 100)

EXCHANGES
3 Lean Meat
1 Vegetable

POINTS
4

PER SERVING
181 Calories
4.4g Carbohydrate
6.0g Fat (2.1g saturated)
0.9g Fiber
26.3g Protein
66mg Cholesterol
78mg Sodium
13mg Calcium
3.4mg Iron

1	(8-ounce) package sliced fresh mushrooms, divided
1	pound lean ground round
2	teaspoons instant minced onion
2	teaspoons low-sodium Worcestershire sauce
1	teaspoon freshly ground pepper
	Vegetable cooking spray
¼	cup dry red wine or canned no-salt-added beef broth
¼	cup water

1. Coarsely chop 1½ cups sliced mushrooms. Combine beef, chopped mushrooms, onion, and Worcestershire sauce in a bowl; shape into 4 equal patties, ¼ inch thick. Sprinkle pepper evenly on both sides of patties.

2. Coat a 12-inch nonstick skillet with cooking spray, and place over medium-high heat until hot. Add patties, and cook 5 to 6 minutes on each side or until done. Transfer to a serving platter, and keep warm.

3. Add wine, water, and remaining mushrooms to skillet; cook over medium heat, stirring constantly, scraping particles that cling to bottom about 3 minutes or until mushrooms are tender. Pour mushroom mixture over patties. Yield: 4 servings.

Serve with herbed new potatoes and steamed green beans.

Patties thicker than ¼ inch will take longer to cook.

Veal Piccata (photo, page 98)

⅓ cup dry vermouth

2 tablespoons fresh lemon juice (about 1 small)

¼ teaspoon garlic powder

⅛ teaspoon salt

Butter-flavored vegetable cooking spray

½ pound (¼-inch-thick) veal cutlets

2 tablespoons chopped fresh parsley

1. Combine first 4 ingredients, stirring well.

2. Coat a medium nonstick skillet with cooking spray; place over medium-high heat until hot. Add half of veal cutlets to skillet; cook 1 minute on each side. Transfer veal to a serving platter, and keep warm. Recoat skillet with cooking spray, and repeat procedure with remaining veal cutlets.

3. Add vermouth mixture to skillet. Cook over high heat 1 minute, stirring constantly, scraping particles that cling to bottom. Pour sauce over veal; sprinkle with parsley, and serve immediately. Yield: 2 servings.

Serve with angel hair pasta and steamed asparagus.

You can substitute pork medaillons or boneless chicken breasts for the veal cutlets, though you may have to cook them a little longer. Be sure to flatten or pound both pork or chicken to about ¼ inch thickness.

EXCHANGES

3 Very Lean Meat

POINTS

3

PER SERVING

143 Calories

3.2g Carbohydrate

3.6g Fat (1.0g saturated)

0.1g Fiber

23.1g Protein

94mg Cholesterol

243mg Sodium

23mg Calcium

1.2mg Iron

Rosemary Grilled Lamb Chops

EXCHANGES
4 Lean Meat

POINTS
6

PER SERVING
241 Calories
3.6g Carbohydrate
10.7g Fat (3.6g saturated)
0.4g Fiber
31.5g Protein
99mg Cholesterol
89mg Sodium
43mg Calcium
2.7mg Iron

¼   cup balsamic vinegar
1   tablespoon lemon juice
1   tablespoon dried rosemary, crushed
¼   teaspoon garlic powder
¼   teaspoon ground pepper
4   (4-ounce) lean lamb loin chops (1 inch thick)
Vegetable cooking spray
Additional balsamic vinegar (optional)

1. Combine first 5 ingredients; stir well.

2. Trim fat from chops. Coat grill rack with cooking spray; place on grill over medium-hot coals (350° to 400°). Place chops on rack; grill, covered, 6 minutes on each side or until desired degree of doneness, basting occasionally with vinegar mixture. Serve with balsamic vinegar, if desired. Yield: 2 servings.

Serve with couscous, roasted asparagus, and crusty bread.

If you have time, marinate the chops 1 to 2 hours in the refrigerator, and the chops will be even more flavorful.

Sweet-Hot Pork Medaillons

1   pound pork tenderloin
⅛   teaspoon dried crushed red pepper
⅛   teaspoon garlic powder
Vegetable cooking spray
1   teaspoon sesame oil
2   tablespoons water
2   tablespoons reduced-sodium soy sauce
2   tablespoons brown sugar

1. Trim fat from pork. Cut pork into 1-inch-thick slices. Place slices between two sheets of heavy-duty plastic wrap, and flatten to ½-inch thickness, using a meat mallet or rolling pin. Sprinkle with pepper and garlic powder.

2. Coat a large nonstick skillet with cooking spray; add oil. Place skillet over medium-high heat until hot. Add half of pork medaillons, and cook 3 minutes on each side or until browned. Remove pork from skillet; set aside, and keep warm. Repeat procedure with remaining half of pork medaillons.

3. Add water, soy sauce, and brown sugar to skillet. Reduce heat to medium; cook, stirring constantly, 1 minute or until bubbly. Spoon sauce over pork. Yield: 4 servings.

Serve with roasted yellow squash and sweet red peppers, and French bread.

> Sesame oil adds a rich, nutty flavor to this recipe, but you can use vegetable oil instead.

EXCHANGES
3½ Very Lean Meat

POINTS
4

PER SERVING
160 Calories
5.1g Carbohydrate
4.1g Fat (1.1g saturated)
0.0g Fiber
24.2g Protein
74mg Cholesterol
299mg Sodium
13mg Calcium
1.7mg Iron

Pork Medaillons with Mustard Sauce

EXCHANGES
3½ Very Lean Meat

POINTS
4

PER SERVING
160 Calories
2.4g Carbohydrate
4.7g Fat (1.2g saturated)
0.2g Fiber
24.9g Protein
74mg Cholesterol
295mg Sodium
50mg Calcium
1.6mg Iron

1   pound pork tenderloin
Vegetable cooking spray
1   teaspoon vegetable oil
½   cup fat-free milk
2   tablespoons Dijon mustard
3   green onions, sliced

1. Trim fat from pork. Cut pork into 1-inch-thick slices. Place slices between two sheets of heavy-duty plastic wrap, and flatten to ½-inch thickness, using a meat mallet or rolling pin.

2. Coat a large nonstick skillet with cooking spray; add oil, and place skillet over medium-high heat until hot. Add half of pork medaillons, and cook 3 minutes on each side or until browned. Remove pork from skillet; set aside, and keep warm. Repeat procedure with remaining half of pork medaillons.

3. Reduce heat to low; add milk to skillet, stirring constantly, scraping particles that cling to bottom. Stir in mustard and green onions. Return pork to skillet; cover and cook 2 minutes, turning to coat with sauce. Yield: 4 servings.

Serve with polenta and steamed broccoli.

> Change the flavor of this recipe by substituting different flavors of mustard such as brown, sweet-hot, or honey mustard.

Marmalade Pork Chops

Vegetable cooking spray

1   teaspoon olive oil

4   (4-ounce) lean boneless pork loin chops, trimmed

2   teaspoons lemon-pepper seasoning

2   tablespoons cider vinegar

¼   cup low-sugar orange marmalade

EXCHANGES

3 Lean Meat

½ Starch

POINTS

5

PER SERVING

221 Calories

7.1g Carbohydrate

9.4g Fat (3.0g saturated)

0.0g Fiber

25.1g Protein

71mg Cholesterol

245mg Sodium

6mg Calcium

1.0mg Iron

1. Coat a large nonstick skillet with cooking spray; add oil, and place over medium-high heat until hot. Sprinkle chops on both sides with lemon-pepper seasoning; add chops to skillet, and cook 5 minutes on each side or until done. Remove from pan, and keep warm.

2. Add vinegar to skillet; stir in marmalade. Return chops to skillet, turning once to coat; cook 1 minute or until thoroughly heated. Serve immediately. Yield: 4 servings.

Serve with green beans and a Waldorf salad.

If you're watching sodium, look for salt-free lemon-herb seasoning. The flavor is similar to lemon-pepper seasoning, but without the salt.

Pineapple-Glazed Pork Chops (photo, right)

EXCHANGES
3 Lean Meat
1 Starch

POINTS
5

PER SERVING
226 Calories
11.0g Carbohydrate
8.3g Fat (2.8g saturated)
0.1g Fiber
25.2g Protein
71mg Cholesterol
224mg Sodium
22mg Calcium
1.2mg Iron

4   (4-ounce) lean boneless pork loin chops, trimmed
¼   teaspoon salt
¼   teaspoon ground pepper
Vegetable cooking spray
1   (6-ounce) can unsweetened pineapple juice
2   tablespoons dry sherry (optional)
2   tablespoons brown sugar
1   teaspoon dried rosemary, crushed
¼   teaspoon garlic powder

To crush dried rosemary, chop it finely with a knife or use a mortar and pestle to crush it.

1. Press pork chops with palm of hand to flatten slightly; sprinkle with salt and pepper.

2. Coat a large nonstick skillet with cooking spray, and place over high heat until hot. Add chops, and cook 1 minute on each side or until browned. Reduce heat to medium-high, and cook chops 4 additional minutes on each side or until done. Remove chops from skillet; set aside, and keep warm.

3. Add pineapple juice and remaining 4 ingredients to skillet, stirring well. Cook over high heat, stirring constantly, scraping particles that cling to bottom. Cook 5 minutes or until juice mixture is thickened.

4. Return chops to skillet, turning to coat with glaze; serve immediately. Yield: 4 servings.

Serve with couscous and baby carrots.

**Gingered Beef
Stir-Fry**
(recipe, page 86)

Veal Piccata
(recipe, page 91)

**Peppered Filets with
Mushroom Sauce**
(recipe, page 88)

Peppery Mushroom Burgers
(recipe, page 90)

Sirloin Steak with Garlic Sauce
(recipe, page 85)

Southwestern Pork Chops

Vegetable cooking spray
4   (4-ounce) lean boneless pork loin chops, trimmed
⅓   cup salsa
2   tablespoons fresh lime juice
¼   cup chopped fresh cilantro or parsley (optional)

1. Coat a large nonstick skillet with cooking spray; place over high heat until hot. Press chops with palm of hand to flatten slightly; add to skillet and cook 1 minute on each side or until browned. Reduce heat to medium-low.

2. Combine salsa and lime juice; pour over chops. Simmer, uncovered, 8 minutes or until chops are done. If desired, sprinkle chops with cilantro. Yield: 4 servings.

Serve with black beans, pineapple wedges, and fresh strawberries.

The strong lemonlike flavor of cilantro is traditional in south-western cuisine, but you can always substitute parsley if cilantro is unavailable.

EXCHANGES
3 Lean Meat

POINTS
4

PER SERVING
190 Calories
2.0g Carbohydrate
8.3g Fat (2.8g saturated)
0.6g Fiber
25.3g Protein
71mg Cholesterol
132mg Sodium
21mg Calcium
1.3mg Iron

Maple-Glazed Ham

EXCHANGES

2 Lean Meat
½ Starch

POINTS

3

PER SERVING

129 Calories
9.2g Carbohydrate
4.1g Fat (0.0g saturated)
0.0g Fiber
14.4g Protein
46mg Cholesterol
1111mg Sodium
14mg Calcium
0.7mg Iron

1   (8-ounce) slice lean cooked ham (about ¼ inch thick)
⅛   teaspoon ground pepper
Vegetable cooking spray
2   tablespoons maple syrup
1   teaspoon Dijon mustard
2   teaspoons cider vinegar

1. Cut ham slice into 3 pieces; sprinkle with pepper.

2. Coat a large nonstick skillet with cooking spray; place over medium-high heat until hot. Add ham to skillet, and cook 3 minutes on each side. Transfer ham to a serving platter, and keep warm.

3. Combine maple syrup, mustard, and vinegar in skillet; stir well. Cook over medium heat, stirring constantly, 1 minute or until mixture is smooth and bubbly. Spoon glaze over ham. Yield: 3 servings.

Serve with mashed sweet potatoes and garden peas.

If you're watching your sodium intake, you can use 33⅓%-less-sodium ham. However, be aware that calories and fat are higher in the lower sodium ham.

poultry

Grilled Herbed Chicken

EXCHANGES

3½ Very Lean Meat

POINTS

3

PER SERVING

144 Calories

0.9g Carbohydrate

3.5g Fat (0.9g saturated)

0.2g Fiber

25.8g Protein

70mg Cholesterol

62mg Sodium

31mg Calcium

1.6mg Iron

2½ teaspoons dried Italian seasoning

¼ teaspoon ground pepper

½ cup dry white wine

2 tablespoons lemon juice

1 teaspoon olive oil

6 (4-ounce) skinned, boned chicken breast halves

Vegetable cooking spray

1. Combine first 5 ingredients; set aside half of herb mixture for basting during grilling. Brush remaining half on chicken.

2. Coat grill rack with cooking spray; place on grill over medium-hot coals (350° to 400°). Place chicken on rack; grill, covered, 5 minutes. Turn chicken; brush reserved herb mixture on chicken, and grill 5 additional minutes or until chicken is done. Yield: 6 servings.

Serve with grilled corn on the cob and sliced tomatoes.

> If you have time to marinate the chicken at least 15 minutes, the herb flavor will be even stronger.

Sesame Chicken (photo, page 117)

2   teaspoons sesame seeds
4   (4-ounce) skinned, boned chicken breast halves
Vegetable cooking spray
2   tablespoons honey
2   tablespoons reduced-sodium soy sauce
¼   teaspoon ground ginger

EXCHANGES

3 Very Lean Meat
½ Starch

POINTS

4

PER SERVING

170 Calories
9.6g Carbohydrate
2.3g Fat (0.5g saturated)
0.0g Fiber
27.0g Protein
66mg Cholesterol
317mg Sodium
16mg Calcium
1.1mg Iron

1. Place a large nonstick skillet over medium-high heat until hot. Add sesame seeds, and cook, stirring constantly, 1 to 2 minutes or until seeds are toasted. Remove seeds, and set aside.

2. Place chicken breast halves between two sheets of heavy-duty plastic wrap, and flatten to ¼-inch thickness, using a meat mallet or rolling pin.

3. Coat skillet with cooking spray; place over medium-high heat until hot. Add chicken, and cook 3 minutes on each side or until chicken is lightly browned.

4. Combine toasted sesame seeds, honey, soy sauce, and ginger; pour over chicken, and cook 1 additional minute, turning chicken to coat with sauce. Serve sauce over chicken. Yield: 4 servings.

Serve with rice and steamed broccoli.

> Serve Sesame Chicken on hoagie rolls with lettuce and tomato for a hearty sandwich.

Cranberry-Apricot Chicken (photo on cover)

EXCHANGES

4 Very Lean Meat

1 Fruit

POINTS

4

PER SERVING

213 Calories

18.3g Carbohydrate

2.7g Fat (0.5g saturated)

1.7g Fiber

26.5g Protein

66mg Cholesterol

155mg Sodium

18mg Calcium

0.9mg Iron

Use kitchen scissors to slice the green onions and to chop the apricots. Coat the scissors with cooking spray before chopping the apricots, and the scissors won't get sticky.

4   (4-ounce) skinned, boned chicken breast halves

½   teaspoon ground sage

Olive oil-flavored vegetable cooking spray

1   teaspoon olive oil

⅔   cup canned reduced-sodium chicken broth, divided

1   teaspoon cornstarch

⅓   cup sweetened dried cranberries (such as Craisins)

⅓   cup chopped dried apricot halves

⅓   cup sliced green onions (about 2 medium)

1. Place chicken breast halves between two sheets of heavy-duty plastic wrap, and flatten to ¼-inch thickness, using a meat mallet or rolling pin. Sprinkle sage evenly over chicken.

2. Coat a large nonstick skillet with cooking spray; add oil, and place over medium-high heat until hot. Add chicken, and cook 3 minutes on each side or until chicken is lightly browned.

3. Combine 1 tablespoon broth and cornstarch; stir well, and set aside. Add cranberries, apricot, and remaining broth to skillet. Bring mixture to a boil; cover, reduce heat, and simmer 6 minutes or until chicken and fruit are tender. Transfer chicken to a serving platter.

4. Stir cornstarch mixture; add to skillet. Stir in green onions, and cook, stirring constantly, 1 minute or until sauce thickens. Serve sauce over chicken. Yield: 4 servings.

Serve with brown rice and a tossed green salad.

Lemon-Pepper Chicken

Vegetable cooking spray

1 teaspoon olive oil

4 (4-ounce) skinned, boned chicken breast halves

1¼ teaspoons lemon–pepper seasoning

¼ cup canned reduced-sodium chicken broth

¼ cup balsamic vinegar

1. Coat a large nonstick skillet with cooking spray; add oil, and place over medium-high heat until hot. While skillet heats, sprinkle both sides of chicken breasts evenly with lemon-pepper seasoning. Add chicken to skillet, and cook 4 to 5 minutes on each side or until chicken is done. Transfer chicken to a serving platter, and keep warm.

2. Add broth and vinegar to skillet; cook, stirring constantly, 1 minute or until slightly thickened. Spoon sauce over chicken. Yield: 4 servings.

Serve with couscous and steamed snow peas.

> Use lemon-pepper seasoning or any other lemon-herb seasoning in this recipe. If sodium is a concern, check the ingredient list on the seasoning label. The closer salt is to the beginning of the list, the higher the sodium content.

EXCHANGES
4 Very Lean Meat

POINTS
3

PER SERVING
138 Calories
0.3g Carbohydrate
2.7g Fat (0.5g saturated)
0.0g Fiber
26.2g Protein
66mg Cholesterol
233mg Sodium
13mg Calcium
0.9mg Iron

Crunchy Chicken Roll-Ups

EXCHANGES
3 Very Lean Meat
2½ Starch

POINTS
6

PER SERVING
317 Calories
40.3g Carbohydrate
3.0g Fat (0.8g saturated)
1.8g Fiber
29.4g Protein
70mg Cholesterol
429mg Sodium
19mg Calcium
1.1mg Iron

1   pound skinned, boned chicken breast halves
1   cup alfalfa sprouts
½   cup sliced water chestnuts
½   cup fat-free creamy Italian dressing
4   (8-inch) fat-free flour tortillas
4   green leaf lettuce leaves

1. Add enough water to a large saucepan or Dutch oven to cover chicken. Bring water to a boil over medium-high heat; reduce heat to low. Add chicken, and simmer 10 minutes or until chicken is done. While chicken cooks, combine sprouts, water chestnuts, and dressing in a bowl.

2. Remove chicken from Dutch oven; cool slightly, and chop. Add chopped chicken to sprout mixture, tossing well.

3. Wrap tortillas in plastic wrap, and microwave at HIGH 30 seconds or until heated. Place a lettuce leaf on each tortilla; spoon chicken mixture evenly onto each lettuce leaf. Roll up each tortilla, and serve immediately. Yield: 4 servings.

Serve with a fruit salad of kiwifruit, strawberries, and pineapple.

To add extra flavor to the chicken, cook it in no-salt-added chicken broth or wine instead of water.

Chicken Fajitas

Vegetable cooking spray
1   pound chicken breast tenders, uncooked
1   tablespoon lime juice
4   (8-inch) fat-free flour tortillas
4   green leaf lettuce leaves
¾   cup thick and chunky salsa
¼   cup nonfat sour cream

1. Coat a large nonstick skillet with cooking spray, and place over medium-high heat until hot. Add chicken, and cook 5 minutes or until chicken is done, stirring often. Add lime juice; cook 1 additional minute, tossing chicken well.

2. Wrap tortillas in plastic wrap, and microwave at HIGH 30 seconds or until heated. Place a lettuce leaf on each tortilla; arrange chicken evenly over lettuce. Spoon salsa evenly over chicken; roll up each tortilla. Spoon 1 tablespoon sour cream over each fajita. Serve immediately. Yield: 4 servings.

Serve with black bean soup.

For a stronger southwestern flavor, sprinkle ¼ teaspoon ground cumin or chili powder over the chicken as it cooks.

EXCHANGES
4 Very Lean Meat
2 Starch

POINTS
6

PER SERVING
308 Calories
30.2g Carbohydrate
3.6g Fat (1.0g saturated)
1.7g Fiber
35.9g Protein
83mg Cholesterol
769mg Sodium
18mg Calcium
1.1mg Iron

Chicken and Vegetables on Pasta

EXCHANGES

3 Very Lean Meat

1 Starch

2 Vegetable

POINTS

5

PER SERVING

265 Calories

26.6g Carbohydrate

3.3g Fat (0.6g saturated)

2.0g Fiber

31.0g Protein

66mg Cholesterol

302mg Sodium

36mg Calcium

1.3mg Iron

3   ounces bow tie pasta, uncooked

Vegetable cooking spray

1   teaspoon olive oil

1   pound skinned, boned chicken breast halves, cut into 1-inch pieces

¾   cup frozen chopped onion

½   teaspoon minced garlic (about 1 clove)

1   cup coarsely chopped zucchini (about 1 small)

2   cups coarsely chopped yellow squash (about 2 small)

1   (14½-ounce) can Italian-style stewed tomatoes, undrained

1. Cook pasta according to package directions, omitting salt and fat.

2. While pasta cooks, coat a large nonstick skillet with cooking spray; add oil, and place over medium-high heat until hot. Add chicken, onion, and garlic. Cook 5 minutes, stirring constantly, or until chicken is browned. Add zucchini, squash, and tomatoes; cook 5 minutes or until vegetables are crisp-tender, stirring occasionally.

3. Drain pasta; arrange on a serving platter. Spoon vegetable mixture over pasta. Yield: 4 servings.

Serve with crusty French rolls.

Substitute any similar size pasta for bow tie like penne, ziti, radiatore, gnocchi, or fusilli.

Peachy Chicken and Rice

1   regular size bag quick-cooking boil-in-bag rice, uncooked, or
        2 cups cooked rice (cooked without salt and fat)

Vegetable cooking spray

1   pound skinned, boned chicken breast halves, cut into 1-inch pieces

½   cup chopped onion (about 1 small)

1   cup chopped green pepper (about 1 large)

1   (8-ounce) can sliced water chestnuts, drained

⅓   cup barbecue sauce

⅓   cup low-sugar peach preserves

2   tablespoons reduced-sodium soy sauce

1. Cook rice according to package directions, omitting salt and fat.

2. While rice cooks, coat a large nonstick skillet with cooking spray, and place over medium-high heat until hot. Add chicken, onion, and pepper; cook 5 minutes or until chicken is lightly browned and vegetables are crisp-tender. Add water chestnuts and remaining 3 ingredients to skillet. Cover, reduce heat, and simmer 10 minutes.

3. Drain rice; remove from bag, and arrange on a serving platter. Spoon chicken mixture over rice. Yield: 4 servings.

Serve with soft dinner rolls.

This recipe is even more attractive if you use 1 small sweet red pepper and 1 small green pepper. Red peppers are usually more expensive, but they have a sweeter, more mellow flavor than the green ones.

EXCHANGES
3 Very Lean Meat
3 Starch

POINTS
7

PER SERVING
337 Calories
46.3g Carbohydrate
2.3g Fat (0.5g saturated)
1.8g Fiber
29.8g Protein
66mg Cholesterol
496mg Sodium
37mg Calcium
2.7mg Iron

Chicken Cacciatore (photo, page 118)

EXCHANGES
3 Very Lean Meat
2 Starch
2 Vegetable

POINTS
7

PER SERVING
340 Calories
39.6g Carbohydrate
5.5g Fat (0.9g saturated)
3.1g Fiber
28.9g Protein
66mg Cholesterol
634mg Sodium
24mg Calcium
2.0mg Iron

1   regular size bag quick-cooking boil-in-bag rice, uncooked, or 2
       cups cooked rice (cooked without salt and fat)
Vegetable cooking spray
1   teaspoon olive oil
1   pound skinned, boned chicken breast halves, cut into 1-inch pieces
1   cup frozen chopped green pepper
1   (14-ounce) jar chunky tomato, garlic, and onion pasta sauce
½   cup water
¼   teaspoon salt

1. Cook rice according to package directions, omitting salt and fat.

2. While rice cooks, coat a large nonstick skillet with cooking spray; add oil, and place over medium-high heat until hot. Add chicken and green pepper; cook, stirring constantly, 5 minutes or until chicken is lightly browned.

3. Add pasta sauce, water, and salt to chicken mixture; bring to a boil. Cover, reduce heat, and simmer 5 minutes.

4. Drain rice, and remove from bag; add to chicken mixture, stirring well. Yield: 4 servings.

Serve with a tossed green salad and crusty French bread.

Quick-cooking boil-in-bag rice cooks in just 10 minutes. For more rice-cooking tips see page 15 in Just the Basics chapter.

Chicken and Couscous Toss

1   cup canned reduced-sodium chicken broth
1¼   cups uncooked couscous
1   large sweet red pepper, cut into 1-inch pieces
½   cup sliced green onions (about 2 large)
½   teaspoon garlic powder
¾   pound skinned, roasted chicken breast (about 4 breast halves)
½   cup red wine vinegar
1½   teaspoons dried basil or oregano

1. Bring broth to a boil in a small saucepan; add couscous. Cover and remove from heat; let stand 5 minutes.

2. While couscous stands, combine red pepper and green onions in a large microwave-safe bowl. Cover bowl with plastic wrap, turning back a small portion of wrap to vent; microwave at HIGH 4 minutes or until vegetables are crisp-tender. Drain well; sprinkle with garlic powder.

3. Remove chicken from bone, and cut into 1-inch pieces.

4. Fluff couscous with a fork. Add couscous, chicken, vinegar, and basil to pepper mixture; toss well. Cover with plastic wrap, and microwave at HIGH 1 to 2 minutes or just until heated. Serve immediately. Yield: 5 servings.

Serve with sliced tomatoes, sliced cucumbers, and garlic bread.

For convenience, we used two packages of Tyson boneless, skinless roasted chicken breasts. You can find this product in the meat section with precooked foods. You can also use deli-roasted chicken or roast your own. Instructions are on page 13 in Just the Basics chapter.

EXCHANGES
3 Very Lean Meat
2 Starch
1 Vegetable

POINTS
5

PER SERVING
274 Calories
36.2g Carbohydrate
2.6g Fat (2.0g saturated)
2.4g Fiber
27.0g Protein
56mg Cholesterol
566mg Sodium
14mg Calcium
1.5mg Iron

Southwestern Chicken Hash

EXCHANGES
3 Very Lean Meat

3 Starch

POINTS
6

PER SERVING
338 Calories

46.8g Carbohydrate

3.5g Fat (0.9g saturated)

3.2g Fiber

30.7g Protein

72mg Cholesterol

721mg Sodium

38mg Calcium

2.2mg Iron

Vegetable cooking spray

4   cups southern-style hash brown potatoes

½   cup frozen chopped onion

2⅓   cups chopped cooked chicken breast

1   (14½-ounce) can Mexican-style stewed tomatoes, undrained

1   (8¾-ounce) can whole-kernel corn, drained

½   teaspoon ground cumin

¼   teaspoon salt

1. Coat a large nonstick skillet with cooking spray; place over medium-high heat until hot. Add potatoes and onion; cook 10 minutes or until browned, stirring often.

2. Add chicken and remaining ingredients to skillet; cook 5 minutes or until thoroughly heated, stirring often. Yield: 4 servings.

Serve with cornbread.

Tyson's frozen chopped cooked chicken is a great time-saver for this recipe, although it's more expensive than cooking it yourself. To cook your own chicken use 1 pound of boneless chicken breast halves for this recipe, and follow the instructions for roasting or poaching chicken breasts on page 13 in Just the Basics chapter.

Barbecue Chicken Pizza (photo, page 118)

Vegetable cooking spray

1 (10-ounce) package refrigerated pizza crust

¾ cup chopped green pepper (about 1 medium)

¾ cup thinly sliced red onion wedges (about 1 small onion)

½ cup honey barbecue sauce

1½ cups shredded cooked chicken breast

1 cup (4 ounces) shredded part-skim mozzarella cheese

EXCHANGES

2 Lean Meat

1 Starch

1 Vegetable

POINTS

5

PER SERVING

238 Calories

21.3g Carbohydrate

5.5g Fat (2.2g saturated)

0.9g Fiber

16.2g Protein

35mg Cholesterol

889mg Sodium

131mg Calcium

0.6mg Iron

1. Coat a 12-inch pizza pan or large baking sheet with cooking spray. Unroll dough, and press into pan. Bake at 425° for 5 minutes or until crust begins to brown.

2. While crust bakes, coat a medium nonstick skillet with cooking spray; place over medium-high heat until hot. Add green pepper and onion, and cook, stirring constantly, 5 minutes or until vegetables are tender.

3. Spread barbecue sauce evenly over baked crust; top evenly with chicken. Arrange vegetable mixture evenly over chicken; sprinkle with cheese. Bake 8 additional minutes or until crust is golden and cheese melts. Yield: 6 servings.

Serve with coleslaw and red grapes.

It's easier and even more flavorful to use roasted chicken available in the supermarket, but the sodium is much higher. Choose from the chicken cooked in the deli or the prepackaged roasted type. Just remember to remove the skin to keep the chicken low fat.

Cranberry-Ginger Grilled Turkey

EXCHANGES

3 Very Lean Meat

1 Starch

½ Fruit

POINTS

5

PER SERVING

226 Calories

23.6g Carbohydrate

3.1g Fat (0.9g saturated)

0.2g Fiber

25.1g Protein

58mg Cholesterol

71mg Sodium

21mg Calcium

1.4mg Iron

1	(8-ounce) can whole-berry cranberry sauce
1	teaspoon ground ginger
1½	teaspoons brown sugar
½	teaspoon dry mustard
¼	teaspoon ground pepper
	Vegetable cooking spray
2	(8-ounce) turkey tenderloins

1. Combine first 5 ingredients, stirring well. Reserve ½ cup cranberry mixture to serve with turkey. Set aside remaining mixture for basting during grilling.

2. Coat grill rack with cooking spray; place on grill over medium-hot coals (350° to 400°). Place tenderloins on rack, and grill, uncovered, 8 to 10 minutes on each side or until meat thermometer registers 170°, basting often with cranberry mixture.

3. Slice tenderloins diagonally across grain into thin slices. Bring reserved ½ cup cranberry mixture to a boil in a small saucepan. Serve with tenderloin slices. Yield: 4 servings.

Serve with brown rice and steamed green beans.

Try this recipe with boneless chicken breast halves. Just cook the chicken for only 5 minutes on each side or until it's done.

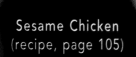

Sesame Chicken
(recipe, page 105)

Chicken Cacciatore
(recipe, page 112)

Barbecue Chicken Pizza
(recipe, page 115)

Turkey Sausage with Peppers
(recipe, page 124)

Turkey Cutlets in Orange Sauce (photo, left)

2   teaspoons vegetable oil
1   pound turkey cutlets
2   tablespoons all-purpose flour
⅓   cup sliced green onions (about 2 medium)
⅛   teaspoon garlic powder
¾   cup unsweetened orange juice
1   tablespoon reduced-sodium soy sauce
Orange slices (optional)

EXCHANGES
4 Very Lean Meat
½ Fruit

POINTS
4

PER SERVING
190 Calories
8.8g Carbohydrate
4.1g Fat (1.0g saturated)
0.3g Fiber
27.7g Protein
68mg Cholesterol
194mg Sodium
23mg Calcium
1.7mg Iron

1. Add oil to a large nonstick skillet, and place over high heat until hot. While skillet heats, dredge turkey cutlets in flour. Add turkey to hot skillet, and cook 3 minutes or until browned, turning once. Remove turkey from skillet.

2. Reduce heat to medium-high; add green onions and garlic powder; cook, stirring constantly, 30 seconds. Add orange juice and soy sauce to skillet; bring to a boil. Cook, stirring constantly, 2 minutes or until mixture thickens slightly.

3. Return turkey to skillet; simmer 2 minutes or until turkey is thoroughly heated. Transfer to a serving platter. Garnish with orange slices, if desired. Yield: 4 servings.

Serve with orzo and steamed snow peas.

The orange sauce in this recipe is delicious with chicken or pork, too. Instead of turkey cutlets, substitute flattened boneless chicken breast halves or pork tenderloin slices.

Lemon Turkey and Asparagus

EXCHANGES
4 Very Lean Meat
1 Vegetable

POINTS
4

PER SERVING
190 Calories
7.4g Carbohydrate
4.2g Fat (1.0g saturated)
1.4g Fiber
28.8g Protein
68mg Cholesterol
318mg Sodium
18mg Calcium
1.9mg Iron

½   cup canned reduced-sodium chicken broth
2   tablespoons lemon juice
1   tablespoon reduced-sodium soy sauce
2   teaspoons cornstarch
¼   teaspoon ground pepper
Vegetable cooking spray
2   teaspoons vegetable oil, divided
1   (9-ounce) package frozen asparagus cuts, thawed
1   small sweet red pepper, chopped
1   pound turkey breast tenderloin, cut into 1-inch pieces

1. Combine first 5 ingredients, stirring well; set aside. Place a large nonstick skillet coated with cooking spray over medium-high heat until hot; add 1 teaspoon oil. Add asparagus and red pepper; cook, stirring constantly, 2 minutes or until tender. Transfer to a bowl; set aside, and keep warm.

2. Add remaining 1 teaspoon oil and turkey to skillet. Cook 3 minutes or until turkey is browned, stirring occasionally. Add broth mixture to skillet; cook 2 minutes or until mixture is thickened and bubbly. Return asparagus mixture to skillet. Stir just until coated. Yield: 4 servings.

Serve with rice and dinner rolls.

Thaw the asparagus in the microwave while you combine the chicken broth mixture, chop the pepper, and cut the turkey.

Turkey Patties with Piquant Sauce

1   pound freshly ground raw turkey

½   cup chopped purple onion (about 1 small)

1   tablespoon dried parsley flakes

2   tablespoons plain nonfat yogurt

Vegetable cooking spray

2   tablespoons brown sugar

2   tablespoons reduced-calorie ketchup

1   teaspoon dry mustard

1. Combine first 4 ingredients in a large bowl, mixing well. Shape mixture into 4 patties.

2. Place patties on rack of a broiler pan coated with cooking spray; broil 3 inches from heat (with electric oven door partially opened) 4 to 5 minutes on each side or until done.

3. While patties broil, combine sugar, ketchup, and dry mustard, stirring well. Spread mixture evenly over tops of patties; broil 30 additional seconds or just until ketchup mixture begins to bubble. Yield: 4 servings.

Serve with steamed green beans and baby carrots.

EXCHANGES

3½ Very Lean Meat

½ Starch

POINTS

4

PER SERVING

177 Calories

7.0g Carbohydrate

4.5g Fat (1.4g saturated)

0.3g Fiber

25.4g Protein

64mg Cholesterol

69mg Sodium

43mg Calcium

1.8mg Iron

The thicker the patties, the longer it will take them to cook.

Turkey Sausage with Peppers (photo, page 119)

EXCHANGES
2 Medium-Fat Meat
2 Vegetable

POINTS
5

PER SERVING
242 Calories
15.0g Carbohydrate
11.2g Fat (3.1g saturated)
3.8g Fiber
21.2g Protein
90mg Cholesterol
650mg Sodium
27mg Calcium
2.1mg Iron

8 ounces Italian turkey sausage (about 2 links)
Vegetable cooking spray
1 medium onion, sliced
1 medium-size green pepper, sliced
1 medium-size sweet red pepper, sliced
⅓ cup dry white wine

1. Remove and discard casings from sausage. Cut sausage into 1½-inch pieces.

2. Coat a large nonstick skillet with cooking spray, and place over medium-high heat until hot. Add sausage, onion, and peppers; cook 8 to 10 minutes or until sausage is browned and vegetables are tender, stirring occasionally.

3. Add wine to skillet. Bring to a boil; reduce heat, and simmer 2 to 3 minutes or until sauce is slightly thickened, stirring occasionally. Yield: 2 servings.

Serve with rice and French bread slices.

You can substitute other types of low-fat turkey sausage for Italian style. Italian turkey sausages often have a strong taste of fennel seeds, a spice with a licorice-like flavor.

salads

Crisp Apple and Cranberry Salad

EXCHANGES

2 Fruit

½ Fat

POINTS

2

PER SERVING

159 Calories

33.6g Carbohydrate

2.6g Fat (0.2g saturated)

6.5g Fiber

2.5g Protein

0mg Cholesterol

80mg Sodium

61mg Calcium

0.3mg Iron

3   Red Delicious apples or firm ripe pears, unpeeled and cored

1   (8-ounce) carton lemon low-fat yogurt

⅓   cup finely chopped celery (about 1 rib)

½   cup sweetened dried cranberries (such as Craisins)

2   tablespoons chopped walnuts

⅛   teaspoon salt

¼   teaspoon freshly ground pepper

1. Cut each apple into 8 wedges; cut crosswise into chunks. Set aside.

2. Combine yogurt and remaining 5 ingredients, stirring well. Add apple, and toss to combine. Yield: 6 servings.

Serve with grilled pork tenderloin, brown rice, and steamed green beans.

> Look for dried cranberries in the produce section or on the grocery shelf near raisins. Check the label; some brands use more sugar than others, which increases the calories.

Melon Wedges with Raspberry Dressing

1 medium honeydew or cantaloupe (about 3 pounds)
2 tablespoons no-sugar-added raspberry spreadable fruit
2 tablespoons vanilla low-fat yogurt
2 tablespoons raspberry vinegar
½ cup fresh raspberries

1. Peel and seed melon, and cut into 20 wedges. Arrange wedges on each of five individual salad plates. Set aside.

2. Combine spreadable fruit, yogurt, and vinegar in a small bowl; stir with a wire whisk until smooth. Spoon dressing over wedges; sprinkle with raspberries. Yield: 5 servings.

Serve with chicken salad and breadsticks.

For a no-mess way to seed cantaloupe or honeydew, use an ice cream scoop or melon baller to scrape seeds from the melon halves.

EXCHANGES

2 Fruit

POINTS

2

PER SERVING

126 Calories
29.9g Carbohydrate
0.9g Fat (0.5g saturated)
4.3g Fiber
2.8g Protein
0mg Cholesterol
29mg Sodium
44mg Calcium
0.6mg Iron

Gazpacho Salad

EXCHANGES

2 Vegetable

POINTS

0

PER SERVING

45 Calories

9.9g Carbohydrate

0.6g Fat (0.1g saturated)

2.4g Fiber

1.7g Protein

0mg Cholesterol

133mg Sodium

18mg Calcium

1.0mg Iron

3   medium-size ripe tomatoes, cut into wedges

1   cup peeled, thinly sliced cucumber (about 1 medium)

¾   cup chopped sweet yellow pepper (about 1 small)

2   cloves garlic, crushed

3   tablespoons fat-free Italian dressing

1. Combine all ingredients in a medium bowl, stirring well. Serve immediately or cover and chill up to 8 hours, if desired. Yield: 4 servings.

Serve with chicken tacos.

If you don't have a garlic press to crush the garlic, place the flat edge of a large knife over unpeeled cloves, and press firmly. Remove the papery skin, and crush again.

Asparagus-Blue Cheese Salad

1   pound fresh asparagus
8   red leaf lettuce leaves
¼   cup fresh lemon juice
3   tablespoons fat-free raspberry vinaigrette
2   ounces crumbled blue cheese

1. Snap off tough ends of asparagus spears. Remove scales from spears with a knife or vegetable peeler, if desired. Place asparagus in a large skillet; add water to cover. Bring to a boil over high heat. Partially cover asparagus, and reduce heat to medium-low; simmer 4 minutes or until asparagus is crisp-tender. Plunge asparagus into ice water; drain.

2. While asparagus simmers, place 2 lettuce leaves on each of four individual salad plates; arrange asparagus spears over lettuce. Set aside.

3. Whisk together lemon juice and vinaigrette in a small bowl. Drizzle lemon juice mixture over salad; sprinkle evenly with cheese. Yield: 4 servings.

Serve with grilled beef tenderloin and roasted potatoes.

The strong flavor of blue cheese is what makes this salad out of the ordinary. Use any variety of blue cheese such as Gorgonzola, Roquefort, or Stilton.

EXCHANGES
2 Vegetable
1 Fat

POINTS
2

PER SERVING
89 Calories
8.8g Carbohydrate
4.4g Fat (2.7g saturated)
1.0g Fiber
5.3g Protein
11mg Cholesterol
276mg Sodium
95mg Calcium
0.7mg Iron

Fruit and Honey Spinach Salad (photo, page 138)

EXCHANGES

1 Fruit

1 Vegetable

⅓ cup white balsamic vinegar

2 tablespoons honey

6 cups ready-to-eat salad spinach leaves, torn (about ½ of a 10-ounce package)

POINTS

1

1 firm ripe mango, peeled, pitted, and cut into thin slices

1 cup fresh raspberries or blueberries

PER SERVING

83 Calories

20.6g Carbohydrate

0.4g Fat (0.1g saturated)

4.7g Fiber

1.6g Protein

0mg Cholesterol

29mg Sodium

47mg Calcium

1.3mg Iron

1. Combine vinegar and honey in a small bowl, stirring well with a wire whisk. Place spinach in a large bowl; pour ¼ cup vinegar mixture over spinach, and toss well.

2. Arrange spinach mixture evenly on each of four individual salad plates. Arrange mango slices and raspberries over spinach; drizzle remaining vinegar mixture over salads. Yield: 4 servings.

Serve with grilled fish and steamed yellow squash.

To save time, look for sliced mango in a jar. It's usually in the produce section of the supermarket.

Fig and Blue Cheese Salad (photo, page 3)

4   cups torn red leaf lettuce

3   tablespoons rice wine vinegar

1   teaspoon extra-virgin olive oil

8   fresh ripe figs or dried figs, quartered

2   ounces crumbled blue cheese

Freshly ground pepper

1. Place lettuce in a large bowl; set aside. Combine vinegar and oil in a small bowl, stirring well with a wire whisk. Pour dressing over lettuce, tossing well.

2. Arrange salad mixture evenly on each of four individual salad plates. Arrange figs evenly over salads; sprinkle with cheese. Sprinkle with pepper. Serve immediately. Yield: 4 servings.

Serve with beef tenderloin and roasted asparagus.

Instead of figs, you can substitute 2 sliced fresh peaches or Red Delicious apples, or 4 sliced fresh apricots.

EXCHANGES

1 Fruit

1 Vegetable

1 Fat

POINTS

2

PER SERVING

142 Calories

21.4g Carbohydrate

5.6g Fat (2.9g saturated)

4.4g Fiber

4.3g Protein

11mg Cholesterol

203mg Sodium

135mg Calcium

1.0mg Iron

Asian Flavors Salad

EXCHANGES
½ Fruit
2 Vegetable

POINTS
2

PER SERVING
84 Calories
16.2g Carbohydrate
1.3g Fat (0.2g saturated)
1.1g Fiber
1.2g Protein
0mg Cholesterol
13mg Sodium
22mg Calcium
0.9mg Iron

6	cups torn romaine lettuce
1	(8-ounce) can sliced water chestnuts, drained
1	(11-ounce) can mandarin oranges, drained
¼	cup rice wine vinegar
1	teaspoon dark sesame oil

1. Combine lettuce, water chestnuts, and oranges in a large bowl; set aside.

2. Combine vinegar and oil in a small bowl, stirring well with a wire whisk. Pour vinegar mixture over salad mixture, tossing well. Serve immediately or cover and chill up to 1 hour, if desired. Yield: 4 servings.

Serve with sweet-and-sour chicken and rice.

> Dark sesame oil has a stronger flavor than the lighter colored type, so you get more flavor from a smaller amount of the dark sesame oil.

Mediterranean Tossed Salad

6 cups torn green leaf lettuce

½ cup thinly sliced purple onion (about 1 small)

¼ cup sliced ripe olives

2 ounces crumbled feta cheese with basil and tomato

1 teaspoon dried oregano

⅓ cup fat-free vinaigrette

1. Combine lettuce, onion, olives, cheese, and oregano in a large bowl; pour vinaigrette over salad, and toss gently. Serve immediately. Yield: 4 servings.

Serve with broiled lamb loin chops, couscous, and French rolls.

If the basil-and-tomato-feta cheese isn't available, substitute peppercorn feta or plain feta.

EXCHANGES

1 Vegetable

1 Fat

POINTS

1

PER SERVING

67 Calories

4.9g Carbohydrate

4.1g Fat (2.1g saturated)

1.3g Fiber

3.3g Protein

10mg Cholesterol

222mg Sodium

45mg Calcium

1.1mg Iron

Barley, Corn, and Feta Salad

EXCHANGES
4 Starch
2 Vegetable
1 Fat

POINTS
5

PER SERVING
345 Calories
70.1g Carbohydrate
5.1g Fat (1.4g saturated)
12.9g Fiber
10.2g Protein
5mg Cholesterol
562mg Sodium
61mg Calcium
2.4mg Iron

This salad serves as a hearty one-dish meal.

2	cups water
1¼	cups quick-cooking barley, uncooked
1	(10-ounce) package frozen corn
2	teaspoons olive oil
¼	cup lemon juice
¾	teaspoon salt
¼	teaspoon ground pepper
½	cup chopped fresh basil
2	tablespoons crumbled feta cheese
¼	cup canned vegetable broth
4	green leaf lettuce leaves
2	large ripe tomatoes, cut into wedges

1. Bring water to a boil in a large saucepan; add barley. Cover, reduce heat, and simmer 8 minutes. Add frozen corn; cover and cook 6 minutes or until barley is tender. Remove from heat; let stand 5 minutes.

2. While barley mixture stands, combine oil and next 6 ingredients in a small bowl; set aside. Arrange lettuce on each of four individual serving plates, and set aside.

3. Add olive oil mixture to barley mixture, stirring well. Spoon barley mixture evenly onto lettuce; top with tomato wedges. Serve immediately or at room temperature. Yield: 4 servings.

Serve with French baguette slices.

Beef Salad Olé (photo, page 138)

½ cup fat-free Italian dressing

½ teaspoon ground cumin

4 ounces shredded roasted lean beef (about ⅔ cup)

1 (15-ounce) can no-salt-added, fat-free kidney beans or no-salt-added black beans, rinsed and drained

¾ cup (3 ounces) shredded or cubed Monterey Jack cheese with peppers

1 (11-ounce) can Mexican-style corn, drained

1½ cups finely chopped plum tomatoes (about 4 medium)

4 green leaf lettuce leaves

1. Combine dressing and cumin in a large bowl, stirring well. Add beef and next 4 ingredients, tossing gently to combine. Serve immediately or cover and chill up to 8 hours, if desired.

2. To serve, arrange lettuce on each of four individual serving plates. Spoon salad evenly over lettuce. Yield: 4 servings.

Serve with warm fat-free tortillas.

We made this recipe with leftover lean eye-of-round roast. Deli roast beef will be higher in sodium.

EXCHANGES

2 Lean Meat

2 Starch

1 Vegetable

POINTS

5

PER SERVING

260 Calories

33.6g Carbohydrate

5.7g Fat (2.9g saturated)

3.6g Fiber

20.1g Protein

27mg Cholesterol

891mg Sodium

200mg Calcium

2.7mg Iron

Grilled Chicken and Raspberry Salad (photo, right)

EXCHANGES

4 Very Lean Meat
1 Fruit
1 Vegetable

POINTS

4

PER SERVING

238 Calories
16.7g Carbohydrate
3.9g Fat (1.0g saturated)
3.5g Fiber
32.0g Protein
84mg Cholesterol
81mg Sodium
23mg Calcium
1.3mg Iron

Vegetable cooking spray
¼ cup balsamic vinegar
3 tablespoons seedless raspberry jam
4 (4-ounce) skinned, boneless chicken breast halves
1 (10-ounce) package ready-to-eat Italian salad mix
1 cup fresh raspberries
Freshly ground pepper

1. Coat grill rack with cooking spray; place on grill over medium-hot coals (350° to 400°).

2. While grill heats, combine vinegar and jam in a small bowl, stirring with a wire whisk until smooth. Reserve 3 tablespoons vinegar mixture. Brush remaining ¼ cup vinegar mixture evenly over each chicken breast. Place chicken on rack, and grill, covered, 5 minutes on each side or until chicken is done. Set chicken aside.

3. Place lettuce mix in a large bowl; pour reserved 3 tablespoons vinegar mixture over lettuce, and toss well. Arrange lettuce mixture evenly on each of four individual serving plates.

4. Cut chicken crosswise into thin strips; arrange chicken strips evenly on lettuce mixture. Top evenly with raspberries. Sprinkle with pepper. Yield: 4 servings.

Serve with lemon muffins.

Italian salad mix is a combination of romaine lettuce and radicchio. A 10-ounce bag contains about 6 cups.

Beef Salad Olé
(recipe, page 135)

**Fruit and Honey
Spinach Salad**
(recipe, page 130)

Garden Vegetable Wraps
(recipe, page 145)

Shrimp Rémoulade Rolls
(recipe, page 147)

**Fruited Chicken
Salad Pitas**
(recipe, page 150)

Mexico Joes
(recipe, page 148)

Tijuana Chicken Salad

6	cups ready-to-eat garden salad
2	cups shredded roasted chicken breast
½	cup salsa
½	cup low-fat sour cream
2	tablespoons lime juice
4	cups no-oil baked tortilla chips, broken

1. Combine salad and chicken in a large bowl. Combine salsa, sour cream, and lime juice in a small bowl, stirring well. Pour salsa mixture over salad mixture, and toss gently.

2. Sprinkle tortilla chips evenly on each of four individual serving plates. Spoon salad mixture evenly over tortilla chips. Serve immediately. Yield: 4 servings.

Serve with sliced tomatoes.

To roast boneless chicken breasts, follow the instructions on page 13 in the Just the Basics chapter.

EXCHANGES

2 Lean Meat

3 Starch

2 Vegetable

POINTS

8

PER SERVING

391 Calories

55.9g Carbohydrate

7.6g Fat (2.8g saturated)

3.7g Fiber

24.5g Protein

55mg Cholesterol

735mg Sodium

54mg Calcium

0.8mg Iron

Turkey Club Salad

EXCHANGES
2 Lean Meat
1 Starch
1 Vegetable

POINTS
4

PER SERVING
197 Calories
17.0g Carbohydrate
6.6g Fat (2.1g saturated)
3.6g Fiber
18.7g Protein
37mg Cholesterol
840mg Sodium
50mg Calcium
3.1mg Iron

8	cups thinly sliced romaine lettuce
8	ounces smoked turkey, cut into thin strips
1	cup halved cherry tomatoes
2	slices cooked bacon, crumbled
½	cup fat-free blue cheese dressing

1. Combine first 4 ingredients in a large bowl; add salad dressing, and toss well. Yield: 4 servings.

Serve with vegetable soup and fat-free crackers.

Substitute any creamy fat-free dressing, such as Thousand Island or Ranch, for blue cheese dressing, if desired.

sandwiches

French Onion Sandwiches (photo, page 4)

EXCHANGES
1 High-Fat Meat
3 Starch

POINTS
7

PER SERVING
314 Calories
43.4g Carbohydrate
8.3g Fat (3.2g saturated)
1.6g Fiber
16.0g Protein
20mg Cholesterol
447mg Sodium
372mg Calcium
1.6mg Iron

8   (1-ounce) slices French bread
Vegetable cooking spray
2   teaspoons reduced-calorie margarine
1   large onion, very thinly sliced
1½ tablespoons brown sugar
1   cup (4 ounces) shredded reduced-fat Swiss cheese

1. Arrange bread slices on a baking sheet. Bake at 375° for 8 minutes or until lightly toasted. Remove from oven, and leave bread slices on baking sheet.

2. While bread toasts, coat a large heavy saucepan with cooking spray; add margarine, and place over high heat until margarine melts. Add onion, and cook, stirring constantly, 3 minutes or until onion is tender. Add brown sugar, and cook 5 additional minutes or until onion is tender and browned, stirring often.

3. Spoon onion mixture evenly on bread slices; top with cheese. Broil 5½ inches from heat (with electric oven door partially opened) 2 minutes. Serve immediately. Yield: 4 servings.

Serve with tomato soup.

Shave thin slices from an onion with a very sharp chef's knife or cut the onion in half and push slowly through the slicing blade of a food processor.

Garden Vegetable Wraps (photo, page 139)

2   slices turkey bacon

4   (10-inch) flour tortillas

¼   cup roasted garlic-flavored light cream cheese (such as Kraft)

20   fresh basil or spinach leaves, cut into thin strips

2½   cups coarsely chopped tomato (about 2 large)

¾   cup chopped sweet red pepper (about 1 small)

¼   teaspoon freshly ground black pepper

1. Cook bacon in a microwave at HIGH 2 minutes or until crisp; crumble and set aside.

2. Spread 1 side of each tortilla with 1 tablespoon cream cheese. Layer bacon, basil, tomato, and red pepper evenly over cream cheese; sprinkle each with black pepper.

3. Roll up tortillas, jellyroll fashion; wrap bottom halves of sandwiches with parchment paper or aluminum foil. Serve immediately. Yield: 4 servings.

Serve with black bean soup and red grapes.

> You can substitute one 7.25-ounce jar of roasted peppers for ¾ cup sweet red pepper. Just remember that the sodium will be higher.

EXCHANGES

1½ Starch

1 Fat

POINTS

4

PER SERVING

194 Calories

24.2g Carbohydrate

6.1g Fat (2.1g saturated)

2.9g Fiber

6.0g Protein

13mg Cholesterol

461mg Sodium

27mg Calcium

0.9mg Iron

Veggie Sandwiches with Beer-Cheese Sauce

EXCHANGES
1 Medium-Fat Meat
2 Starch

POINTS
4

PER SERVING
221 Calories
31.6g Carbohydrate
5.2g Fat (2.6g saturated)
2.0g Fiber
12.3g Protein
8mg Cholesterol
569mg Sodium
11mg Calcium
0.9mg Iron

Have plenty of napkins on hand when you serve these cheesy, juicy sandwiches; they're messy, but worth it.

4   (2-ounce) onion rolls
Vegetable cooking spray
1   (8-ounce) package sliced fresh mushrooms
1½ cups sliced zucchini (about 1 medium)
3   ounces reduced-fat loaf process cheese spread, cubed (such as Velveeta)
3   tablespoons light beer
⅛   teaspoon ground red pepper

1. Wrap onion rolls in aluminum foil, and bake at 350° for 5 to 7 minutes or until warm.

2. While rolls bake, coat a large nonstick skillet with cooking spray, and place over medium-high heat until hot. Add mushrooms and zucchini, and cook 5 minutes or until vegetables are tender, stirring often.

3. Place cheese spread and beer in a small saucepan; cook over medium heat, stirring constantly, until cheese melts and mixture is smooth. Stir in pepper. Remove from heat.

4. To serve, spoon one-fourth of vegetable mixture onto bottom half of each warm onion roll. Spoon about 2 tablespoons cheese sauce over vegetables; top with remaining roll half. Serve immediately. Yield: 4 servings.

Serve with fresh pineapple spears and strawberries.

Shrimp Rémoulade Rolls (photo, page 139)

3 cups water

1 pound peeled and deveined medium-size fresh shrimp (about 40)

¼ cup Creole mustard

3 tablespoons reduced-fat mayonnaise

3 tablespoons dill pickle relish

¼ teaspoon ground pepper

½ (16-ounce) package twin French bread loaves

6 green leaf lettuce leaves

1. Bring water to a boil in a medium saucepan; add shrimp, and cook 3 to 5 minutes or until shrimp turn pink.

2. While shrimp cooks, combine mustard and next 3 ingredients, and set aside. Split bread loaf in half horizontally; place halves back together, and wrap loaf in aluminum foil. Bake at 425° for 5 minutes or until heated.

3. Drain shrimp well; rinse with cold water. Coarsely chop shrimp; add to mustard mixture, stirring well.

4. Line each cut half of bread loaf with 3 lettuce leaves. Spoon shrimp mixture evenly over lettuce. Cut each half diagonally into 3 slices. Serve immediately. Yield: 6 servings.

Serve with coleslaw.

EXCHANGES
2 Lean Meat

1½ Starch

POINTS
4

PER SERVING
202 Calories

22.6g Carbohydrate

4.2g Fat (0.4g saturated)

1.1g Fiber

16.8g Protein

120mg Cholesterol

610mg Sodium

44mg Calcium

2.8mg Iron

You can save some cooking time by having the shrimp steamed at the grocery store.

Mexico Joes (photo, page 140)

EXCHANGES
2 Lean Meat
2½ Starch

POINTS
6

PER SERVING
284 Calories
31.4g Carbohydrate
7.5g Fat (1.9g saturated)
1.2g Fiber
20.8g Protein
58mg Cholesterol
357mg Sodium
27mg Calcium
2.6mg Iron

Vegetable cooking spray
1 pound ground round
½ cup frozen chopped onion
1 (4.5-ounce) can chopped green chiles, undrained
2 tablespoons 40%-less-sodium taco seasoning
1 (8-ounce) can no-salt-added tomato sauce
6 hamburger buns, warmed

1. Coat a large nonstick skillet with cooking spray; place over high heat until hot. Add ground round and onion; cook 5 minutes until meat is browned and onion is tender, stirring to crumble meat. Add chiles, taco seasoning, and tomato sauce, stirring well. Cook over medium heat 3 to 4 minutes or until thoroughly heated, stirring often.

2. Spoon meat mixture evenly over bottom halves of buns; top with remaining bun halves. Yield: 6 servings.

Serve with no-oil baked tortilla chips and carrot sticks.

> Mix the leftover taco seasoning with nonfat sour cream to serve with fajitas or stir the seasoning into crushed corn flakes to use as a coating for oven-fried chicken.

Roast Beef-Feta Pita Pockets

½ cup plus 2 tablespoons chopped seeded cucumber
⅓ cup fat-free Ranch-style dressing
¼ cup crumbled feta cheese
4 green leaf lettuce leaves
2 (6-inch) pita bread rounds, cut in half
6 ounces very thinly sliced deli roast beef

1. Combine cucumber, dressing, and cheese in a small bowl, stirring well. Place 1 lettuce leaf into each pita half; add 1½ ounces roast beef to each pita pocket. Spoon cucumber mixture evenly into each pocket. Serve immediately. Yield: 4 servings.

Serve with fresh pear wedges.

For a lower sodium sandwich use leftover cooked roast beef instead of sliced deli meat.

EXCHANGES
1 Medium-Fat Meat
1 Starch
1 Vegetable

POINTS
4

PER SERVING
187 Calories
21.6g Carbohydrate
4.3g Fat (3.3g saturated)
2.6g Fiber
13.2g Protein
31mg Cholesterol
821mg Sodium
97mg Calcium
1.0mg Iron

Fruited Chicken Salad Pitas (photo, page 140)

EXCHANGES

2 Very Lean Meat

1 Starch

½ Fruit

POINTS

4

PER SERVING

208 Calories

23.0g Carbohydrate

3.8g Fat (0.7g saturated)

2.7g Fiber

18.5g Protein

46mg Cholesterol

448mg Sodium

34mg Calcium

1.5mg Iron

⅓   cup nonfat mayonnaise

¼   teaspoon salt

2½ cups chopped cooked chicken breast

1   cup halved seedless red grapes

1½ tablespoons chopped pecans, toasted

1   (11-ounce) can mandarin oranges, drained

6   small green leaf lettuce leaves

3   (6-inch) whole wheat pita bread rounds, cut in half crosswise

1. Combine first 5 ingredients in a medium bowl, stirring well. Gently stir in oranges.

2. Place 1 lettuce leaf in each pita pocket half. Spoon ¾ cup chicken salad into each pita half. Yield: 6 servings.

Serve with fat-free pretzels.

In the Just the Basics chapter you'll find instructions for roasting or poaching chicken breast halves (page 13), and for toasting nuts (page 20).

Holiday Turkey Sandwiches

2	tablespoons fat-free cream cheese
2	tablespoons nonfat mayonnaise
8	slices whole wheat sandwich bread
¼	cup cranberry-orange crushed fruit
8	ounces thinly sliced roasted turkey breast
4	green leaf lettuce leaves

EXCHANGES

2 Very Lean Meat

2 Starch

POINTS

5

PER SERVING

257 Calories

33.6g Carbohydrate

3.4g Fat (0.9g saturated)

2.1g Fiber

23.4g Protein

42mg Cholesterol

458mg Sodium

86mg Calcium

1.9mg Iron

1. Combine cream cheese and mayonnaise in a small bowl, stirring until smooth. Spread 1 tablespoon cream cheese mixture on each of 4 slices bread. Spread 1 tablespoon crushed fruit over cream cheese mixture. Top each with 2 ounces turkey and 1 lettuce leaf. Place remaining bread slices over lettuce. Yield: 4 servings.

Serve with pear slices and green grapes.

The flavors in this sandwich will work well with thinly sliced ham or roasted chicken, too.

Italian Turkey Stack

EXCHANGES
1 Medium-Fat Meat
2 Starch

POINTS
5

PER SERVING
228 Calories
29.0g Carbohydrate
5.6g Fat (2.7g saturated)
1.6g Fiber
14.8g Protein
29mg Cholesterol
830mg Sodium
155mg Calcium
1.7mg Iron

4   (1½-ounce) Italian rolls, split
¼   cup fat-free Italian dressing
2   ounces thinly sliced lean cooked turkey ham
2   ounces thinly sliced turkey salami
3   ounces thinly sliced part-skim mozzarella cheese
1   cup thinly sliced roasted red pepper
Freshly ground black pepper

1. Brush cut side of rolls with dressing. Fold turkey ham and salami in half, and layer on bottom halves of rolls. Top with cheese and red pepper; sprinkle with black pepper. Top with remaining roll halves. Serve immediately. Yield: 4 sandwiches.

Serve with minestrone.

Slices of turkey ham and turkey salami are sold prepackaged in the sandwich meats section of the supermarket. If you can't find turkey salami, use 4 ounces of turkey ham.

Breakfast Burritos

4	ounces low-fat smoked turkey sausage (such as Healthy Choice)
⅓	cup sliced green onions (about 2 medium)
1	cup fat-free egg substitute
4	(8-inch) flour tortillas
1	cup (4 ounces) shredded reduced-fat sharp Cheddar cheese
¼	cup salsa

EXCHANGES
2 Medium-Fat Meat
1½ Starch

POINTS
6

PER SERVING
260 Calories
23.0g Carbohydrate
8.5g Fat (3.8g saturated)
1.4g Fiber
21.3g Protein
32mg Cholesterol
785mg Sodium
321mg Calcium
2.4mg Iron

1. Place a large nonstick skillet over medium-high heat until hot. Add sausage and green onions, and cook 5 minutes or until sausage is browned, stirring until it crumbles. Pour egg substitute over sausage mixture. Cook until egg substitute mixture is set, stirring occasionally.

2. Spoon ½ cup egg mixture onto each tortilla; sprinkle evenly with cheese. Fold opposite sides of tortillas over filling. Serve each burrito with 1 tablespoon salsa. Serve immediately. Yield: 4 servings.

Serve with fresh orange slices.

You can substitute turkey breakfast sausage and Italian turkey sausage for smoked turkey sausage. Breakfast sausage is spicier, and Italian sausage is traditionally seasoned with fennel seed.

Pita Pizza

EXCHANGES

1 High-Fat Meat

2 Starch

POINTS

5

PER SERVING

251 Calories

28.7g Carbohydrate

7.5g Fat (2.9g saturated)

5.2g Fiber

12.6g Protein

28mg Cholesterol

786mg Sodium

225mg Calcium

1.6mg Iron

2   tablespoons pizza sauce

1   (6-inch) pita bread round

2   tablespoons shredded part-skim mozzarella cheese

5   slices turkey pepperoni

1. Spread pizza sauce on 1 side of pita, leaving a ½-inch border. Top with cheese and pepperoni. Bake at 450° for 8 minutes or until cheese melts. Yield: 1 serving.

Serve with a tossed green salad.

Store the opened jar of pizza sauce in the refrigerator and the opened package of pepperoni in the freezer; then you'll be ready to make this sandwich at a moment's notice.

side dishes

Broiled Maple Grapefruit

EXCHANGES
1 Fruit

POINTS
1

2   medium grapefruit
3   tablespoons reduced-calorie maple syrup
⅛   teaspoon ground cinnamon
2   teaspoons chopped pecans
Ground cinnamon (optional)

PER SERVING
59 Calories
13.5g Carbohydrate
1.0g Fat (0.1g saturated)
1.0g Fiber
1.0g Protein
0mg Cholesterol
3mg Sodium
19mg Calcium
0.2mg Iron

1. Cut grapefruit in half crosswise; remove seeds. Run a sharp knife or grapefruit knife around each section to loosen from membrane. Place grapefruit, cut side up, on rack of a broiler pan.

2. Combine syrup and ⅛ teaspoon cinnamon; brush mixture evenly over grapefruit halves, and sprinkle with pecans. Broil 5½ inches from heat (with electric oven door partially opened) 5 minutes or until thoroughly heated. Sprinkle with additional cinnamon, if desired. Yield: 4 servings.

Serve with bran muffins and nonfat yogurt for breakfast.

Buy pink grapefruit for sweeter flavored fruit.

Mexican Black Beans
(recipe, page 162)

Cranberry-Glazed Oranges
(recipe, right)

Sugar Snap Peas with Cashews
(recipe, page 164)

Cranberry-Glazed Oranges (photo, top left)

2   tablespoons sliced almonds
4   medium-size navel oranges (about 2½ pounds)
1   (8-ounce) can jellied cranberry sauce
¼   cup unsweetened orange juice
¼   teaspoon ground cinnamon

1. Place a large nonstick skillet over medium-high heat. Add almonds, and cook, stirring constantly, 5 minutes or until toasted. Remove from skillet, and set aside.

2. Peel oranges, and cut crosswise into ¼-inch-thick slices. Set aside.

3. Combine cranberry sauce, orange juice, and cinnamon in a bowl, stirring well with a wire whisk until smooth. Combine cranberry mixture and half of orange slices in skillet. Cook over medium heat 2 minutes or until oranges are thoroughly heated, stirring gently. Remove oranges from skillet, using a slotted spoon; set aside, and keep warm. Repeat procedure with remaining orange slices.

4. Place orange slices and any remaining cranberry mixture in a large serving bowl; sprinkle with toasted almonds. Serve immediately. Yield: 6 servings.

Serve with roasted turkey breast, steamed green beans, and whole wheat rolls.

EXCHANGES

2 Fruit

POINTS

2

PER SERVING

135 Calories
31.0g Carbohydrate
1.2g Fat (0.1g saturated)
6.5g Fiber
1.9g Protein
0mg Cholesterol
19mg Sodium
62mg Calcium
0.3mg Iron

This holiday side dish can double as dessert.

Curried Baked Pineapple

EXCHANGES
½ Starch
1 Fruit

POINTS
2

PER SERVING
118 Calories
24.6g Carbohydrate
1.4g Fat (0.4g saturated)
0.0g Fiber
1.4g Protein
2mg Cholesterol
82mg Sodium
47mg Calcium
0.4mg Iron

2   (20-ounce) cans pineapple chunks in juice, drained
15   reduced-fat round buttery crackers, crushed (such as Ritz)
¼   cup firmly packed brown sugar
¼   cup (1 ounce) shredded reduced-fat sharp Cheddar cheese
½   teaspoon curry powder
Fat-free butter spray

1. Place pineapple chunks in an ungreased 11- x 7- x 1½-inch baking dish; set aside.

2. Combine cracker crumbs and next 3 ingredients, stirring well. Sprinkle cracker mixture over pineapple. Coat cracker mixture with butter spray (about 5 sprays). Bake at 450° for 10 minutes or until lightly browned. Yield: 8 servings.

Serve with roasted chicken and stir-fried green and sweet red peppers.

> We used I Can't Believe It's Not Butter brand butter spray; it adds the taste of butter, but without calories, fat, or cholesterol. You'll find it in your supermarket's dairy case.

Sesame Asparagus and Mushrooms

2   tablespoons rice wine vinegar
1   teaspoon dark sesame oil
¼   teaspoon salt
⅛   teaspoon garlic powder
⅛   teaspoon ground pepper
1   pound fresh asparagus spears
8   ounces whole fresh mushrooms
½   teaspoon sesame seeds (optional)

1. Combine first 5 ingredients in a heavy-duty, zip-top plastic bag.

2. Snap off tough ends of asparagus. Remove scales with a knife or vegetable peeler, if desired. Cut asparagus spears in half. Cut mushrooms into quarters (or in half, if small). Add asparagus, mushrooms, and sesame seeds, if desired, to vinegar mixture; seal bag, and turn to coat vegetables well.

3. Place vegetables in a single layer on a 15- x 10- x 1-inch jellyroll pan. Bake at 500° for 10 minutes or until tender, stirring after 5 minutes. Yield: 6 servings.

Serve with broiled fish and garlic bread.

> Use the heaviest jellyroll pan or roasting pan available for roasting the vegetables.

EXCHANGES
1 Vegetable

POINTS
0

PER SERVING
31 Calories
4.1g Carbohydrate
1.3g Fat (0.2g saturated)
1.5g Fiber
2.0g Protein
0mg Cholesterol
101mg Sodium
18mg Calcium
1.0mg Iron

Mexican Black Beans (photo, page 157)

EXCHANGES
1½ Starch

POINTS
2

PER SERVING
120 Calories
22.1g Carbohydrate
0.5g Fat (0.1g saturated)
4.3g Fiber
7.3g Protein
0mg Cholesterol
407mg Sodium
24mg Calcium
1.7mg Iron

2 (15-ounce) cans fat-free, no-salt-added black beans, drained
1 (14½-ounce) can Mexican-style stewed tomatoes, undrained
1 tablespoon red wine vinegar
1 teaspoon sugar
¼ cup sliced green onions (about 2 large)

1. Combine first 4 ingredients in a large saucepan, stirring well. Cook over medium heat 10 minutes, stirring occasionally. Ladle beans into serving bowls; sprinkle each serving with sliced green onions. Yield: 7 servings.

Serve with beef fajitas and pineapple wedges.

Slice green onions using kitchen scissors; there's less to clean up than slicing the onions with a knife on a cutting board.

Stewed Okra, Corn, and Tomatoes

1   (16-ounce) package frozen vegetable gumbo mixture
1   (14½-ounce) can Cajun-style stewed tomatoes
¼   teaspoon no-salt-added Creole seasoning
3   slices turkey bacon, cooked and crumbled

1. Combine first 3 ingredients in a large saucepan, stirring well. Cover and cook over medium heat 14 minutes or until vegetables are tender. Sprinkle with crumbled bacon. Yield: 5 servings.

Serve with broiled shrimp and rice.

This recipe is supereasy because all you do is "dump and cook." While the vegetables cook, you can cook the bacon in the microwave; it takes 2 to 3 minutes for 3 slices.

EXCHANGES

1 Starch

POINTS

1

PER SERVING

85 Calories

15.9g Carbohydrate

1.2g Fat (0.3g saturated)

3.8g Fiber

3.1g Protein

6mg Cholesterol

478mg Sodium

0mg Calcium

0.0mg Iron

Sugar Snap Peas with Cashews (photo, page 158)

EXCHANGES
1 Starch
½ Fat

POINTS
1

PER SERVING
97 Calories
14.2g Carbohydrate
2.9g Fat (0.5g saturated)
3.5g Fiber
4.5g Protein
0mg Cholesterol
282mg Sodium
60mg Calcium
3.0mg Iron

¼ cup unsweetened orange juice
2 tablespoons reduced-sodium soy sauce
1½ teaspoons cornstarch
Vegetable cooking spray
1 (16-ounce) package frozen Sugar Snap peas
½ cup thinly sliced green onions (about 4 large)
2 tablespoons chopped salted cashews
Orange slices (optional)

1. Combine first 3 ingredients, stirring well. Set aside.

2. Coat a large nonstick skillet with cooking spray; place over medium-high heat until hot. Add peas and green onions, and cook 4 minutes, stirring often. Add orange juice mixture to skillet. Cook, stirring constantly, 1 to 2 minutes or until mixture thickens. Transfer to a serving bowl; sprinkle with cashews. Garnish with orange slices, if desired. Yield: 4 servings.

Serve with chicken teriyaki and rice.

> If you can't find Sugar Snap peas, use frozen snow pea pods.

Mashed Parsley Potatoes (photo, page 176)

1	pound unpeeled round red potatoes (small to medium size)
2	tablespoons water
¼	cup fat-free milk
1½	tablespoons reduced-calorie margarine
1	tablespoon chopped fresh parsley
½	teaspoon seasoned salt
⅛	teaspoon ground pepper

1. Cut potatoes into quarters; place potato and water in a medium-size microwave-safe bowl. Cover tightly with heavy-duty plastic wrap; fold back a small edge of wrap to allow steam to escape. Microwave at HIGH 9 minutes or until tender, stirring after 4 minutes.

2. Drain potato; return to bowl. Add milk and remaining ingredients. Mash with a potato masher or fork until potato is mashed and mixture is combined. Yield: 4 servings.

Serve with meat loaf and steamed green beans.

An easy way to chop fresh parsley is to pack it in a measuring cup and snip it with kitchen scissors until it's chopped.

EXCHANGES
1½ Starch
½ Fat

POINTS
2

PER SERVING
113 Calories
19.8g Carbohydrate
2.9g Fat (0.4g saturated)
2.1g Fiber
3.1g Protein
0mg Cholesterol
305mg Sodium
35mg Calcium
1.6mg Iron

Creamed Spinach

EXCHANGES

2 Vegetable

½ Fat

½ Skim Milk

POINTS

2

PER SERVING

117 Calories

13.7g Carbohydrate

3.2g Fat (1.9g saturated)

3.4g Fiber

9.3g Protein

10mg Cholesterol

430mg Sodium

294mg Calcium

2.3mg Iron

1 (10-ounce) package frozen chopped spinach

3 tablespoons roasted garlic-flavored light cream cheese

Vegetable cooking spray

¼ cup chopped onion (about ¼ small)

¼ cup chopped sweet red pepper (about ¼ small)

¼ teaspoon salt

Dash of ground black pepper

¾ cup evaporated skimmed milk

1. Cook spinach according to package directions, omitting salt; drain well. Combine spinach and cream cheese in a bowl, stirring well.

2. Coat a medium saucepan with cooking spray; place over medium-high heat until hot. Add onion and sweet red pepper, and cook 3 minutes until tender, stirring often. Stir in spinach mixture, salt, and black pepper.

3. Reduce heat to medium-low. Gradually add milk, stirring until smooth. Cook, stirring constantly, 3 to 5 minutes or until mixture is creamy. Yield: 3 servings.

Serve with pork loin chops and steamed carrots.

> If you can't find garlic-flavored light cream cheese, use plain light cream cheese and stir in ⅛ teaspoon garlic powder.

Parmesan Squash and Onions

1¼ pounds yellow squash, sliced (about 4 medium)

½ cup sliced onion (about ½ medium)

½ cup canned low-sodium chicken broth

⅛ teaspoon ground pepper

¼ teaspoon garlic salt

2 tablespoons grated fat-free Parmesan cheese

1. Combine first 5 ingredients in a large saucepan; bring to a boil. Reduce heat, and simmer, uncovered, 12 minutes or until squash is tender, stirring often.

2. Remove squash from pan, using a slotted spoon, and transfer to a serving bowl. Add cheese, and toss gently. Yield: 4 servings.

Serve with spaghetti with tomato sauce and herbed Italian bread.

For a more colorful side dish, use half zucchini squash and half yellow crookneck squash.

EXCHANGES

1 Vegetable

POINTS

0

PER SERVING

36 Calories

7.4g Carbohydrate

0.2g Fat (0.0g saturated)

1.6g Fiber

1.2g Protein

0mg Cholesterol

250mg Sodium

23mg Calcium

0.5mg Iron

Lemon Pasta

EXCHANGES

1½ Starch

POINTS

2

PER SERVING

118 Calories
22.5g Carbohydrate
1.3g Fat (0.2g saturated)
1.0g Fiber
4.1g Protein
0mg Cholesterol
137mg Sodium
10mg Calcium
1.4mg Iron

6 ounces penne (tubular pasta), uncooked (1½ cups)
1 teaspoon garlic-flavored olive oil
1½ cups sliced fresh mushrooms
⅓ cup sliced green onions (about 3 medium)
½ cup dry white wine
½ to 1 teaspoon grated lemon rind
¼ teaspoon salt
½ teaspoon lemon-pepper seasoning

1. Cook pasta according to package directions, omitting salt and fat; drain well.

2. While pasta cooks, add olive oil to a large nonstick skillet; place over medium-high heat until hot. Add mushrooms and green onions, and cook 3 minutes, stirring often. Add wine; cook 5 minutes or until wine is reduced by half. Pour mushroom mixture over pasta; add lemon rind, salt, and lemon-pepper seasoning. Toss well. Serve immediately. Yield: 6 servings.

Serve with grilled fish and a spinach salad.

There will be excess liquid in the skillet when you first add the mushroom mixture, but the pasta absorbs a good bit of it, leaving the pasta well coated.

Linguine with Red Pepper Sauce

8 ounces linguine, uncooked
½ (7.25-ounce) jar roasted sweet red peppers, drained
Vegetable cooking spray
¼ cup sliced green onions (about 2 large)
½ teaspoon minced garlic (1 small clove)
⅓ cup low-fat sour cream
½ cup evaporated skimmed milk
½ teaspoon salt
⅛ teaspoon ground black pepper

EXCHANGES
1½ Starch

POINTS
3

PER SERVING
135 Calories
24.2g Carbohydrate
1.8g Fat (0.8g saturated)
0.8g Fiber
5.3g Protein
4mg Cholesterol
172mg Sodium
65mg Calcium
1.2mg Iron

1. Cook linguine according to package directions, omitting salt and fat; drain well.

2. While linguine cooks, place red peppers in container of an electric blender; cover and process until smooth. Set aside.

3. Coat a medium saucepan with cooking spray; place over medium-high heat until hot. Add green onions and garlic; cook 5 minutes or until tender. Remove from heat; add sour cream and red pepper puree. Gradually add milk, stirring with a wire whisk until blended. Return to heat, and cook, stirring constantly, until smooth and thoroughly heated. Stir in salt and black pepper. Combine linguine and sauce, and toss well. Serve immediately. Yield: 8 servings.

Serve with grilled pork tenderloin and a tossed green salad.

Use as large a pot as possible to cook long strands of pasta, and stir often. The pasta cooks more evenly if it has room to move freely during cooking.

Calico Couscous

EXCHANGES

2 Starch

POINTS

3

PER SERVING

144 Calories

30.9g Carbohydrate

0.5g Fat (0.0g saturated)

2.1g Fiber

5.3g Protein

0mg Cholesterol

242mg Sodium

9mg Calcium

1.1mg Iron

1½ cups water

½   cup frozen whole-kernel corn

1½ tablespoons lime juice

1   teaspoon minced garlic (about 2 cloves)

½   teaspoon salt

¼   teaspoon ground pepper

1   cup couscous, uncooked

¾   cup seeded, chopped tomato (1 medium)

2   tablespoons chopped fresh cilantro or parsley

1. Combine first 6 ingredients in a medium saucepan; place over medium-high heat, and bring to a boil. Stir in couscous; remove from heat, and let stand 5 minutes.

2. Fluff couscous mixture with a fork. Add tomato and cilantro, tossing well. Yield: 5 servings.

Serve with grilled chicken breasts and steamed asparagus.

> Save time by chopping the tomato while the couscous cooks. Slice the tomato in half horizontally, and use a spoon to remove the seeds from the seed pockets.

Skillet Broccoli Rice

2   cups chopped fresh broccoli flowerets
1   (10.75-ounce) can 98% fat-free broccoli-cheese soup
1⅓ cups canned reduced-sodium chicken broth
⅛   teaspoon ground pepper
2   cups instant rice, uncooked

1. Arrange broccoli in a steamer basket over boiling water. Cover and steam 3 to 4 minutes or until broccoli is crisp-tender.

2. Combine soup, broth, and pepper in a large nonstick skillet, stirring with a wire whisk until smooth. Bring to a boil. Stir in rice and broccoli. Cover, reduce heat, and cook 5 to 6 minutes or until liquid is absorbed and rice is tender. Fluff with a fork before serving. Yield: 8 servings.

Serve with broiled beef patties and a Waldorf salad.

You can substitute a 10-ounce package of frozen cut broccoli for 2 cups of fresh broccoli flowerets.

EXCHANGES
1 Starch

POINTS
2

PER SERVING
94 Calories
18.4g Carbohydrate
1.1g Fat (0.5g saturated)
0.6g Fiber
2.8g Protein
3mg Cholesterol
348mg Sodium
24mg Calcium
0.6mg Iron

Quick Spanish Rice

EXCHANGES

1½ Starch

POINTS

2

PER SERVING

108 Calories

23.8g Carbohydrate

0.1g Fat (0.0g saturated)

0.7g Fiber

2.5g Protein

0mg Cholesterol

128mg Sodium

12mg Calcium

1.1mg Iron

1   cup water

1   (8-ounce) can no-salt–added tomato sauce

¾   cup frozen seasoning blend (such as McKenzie's)

½   cup thick and chunky salsa

½   teaspoon chili powder

¼   teaspoon salt

2   cups instant rice, uncooked

1. Combine first 6 ingredients in a medium saucepan; bring to a boil. Stir in rice. Cover, remove from heat, and let stand 5 minutes or until liquid is absorbed and rice is tender. Yield: 8 servings.

Serve with baked chicken quesadillas and a fruit salad.

Frozen seasoning blend is a mix of chopped onions, celery, sweet red peppers, green peppers, and parsley. It's handy to use for soups, stews, and sauces, too.

Fruited Brown Rice

1 cup instant brown rice, uncooked
⅔ cup halved seedless red or green grapes
¼ cup coarsely chopped pecans, toasted
2 tablespoons sherry vinegar or rice wine vinegar
1 teaspoon extra-virgin olive oil
½ teaspoon salt
½ teaspoon ground pepper

1. Cook rice according to package directions, omitting salt and fat.

2. Combine rice, grapes, and pecans in a medium bowl. Stir in vinegar and remaining ingredients. Serve immediately or cover and chill up to 24 hours, if desired. Yield: 5 servings.

Serve with broiled pork loin chops and steamed green beans.

Instructions for toasting nuts are on page 20 in the Just the Basics chapter. You can use 2 cups of leftover cooked brown rice if you have it on hand.

EXCHANGES

1 Starch
½ Fruit
1 Fat

POINTS

3

PER SERVING

157 Calories
24.2g Carbohydrate
5.8g Fat (0.6g saturated)
2.2g Fiber
2.7g Protein
0mg Cholesterol
240mg Sodium
14mg Calcium
0.6mg Iron

Mushroom Barley (photo, right)

EXCHANGES

1½ Starch

POINTS

1

PER SERVING

109 Calories

23.0g Carbohydrate

0.5g Fat (0.1g saturated)

4.7g Fiber

3.4g Protein

0mg Cholesterol

93mg Sodium

15mg Calcium

1.1mg Iron

1   (14¼-ounce) can no-salt-added beef broth

1   tablespoon low-sodium Worcestershire sauce

¼   teaspoon salt

¼   teaspoon ground pepper

1   cup quick-cooking barley, uncooked

Vegetable cooking spray

1   (8-ounce) package sliced fresh mushrooms

¾   cup frozen chopped onion, thawed

½   cup finely chopped celery (about 1 rib)

1. Combine first 4 ingredients in a medium saucepan; bring to a boil. Add barley; cover, reduce heat, and simmer 10 minutes. Remove from heat, and let stand 5 minutes.

2. While barley stands, coat a large nonstick skillet with cooking spray, and place over medium-high heat until hot. Add mushrooms, onion, and celery; cook 3 minutes or until tender, stirring often. Stir into cooked barley. Yield: 8 servings.

Serve with grilled flank steak and roasted yellow and zucchini squash.

Look for barley on the same aisle in the supermarket as rice and other grains.

Mashed Parsley Potatoes
(recipe, page 165)

Southwest Meat Loaf
(recipe, page 181)

from the slow cooker

From the Slow Cooker

Slow cooking makes fast work of dinner. What could be easier than walking in the door after a busy day and spooning a hot cooked meal onto dinner plates a few minutes later? And unlike oven cooking, the cooking times for a slow cooker are flexible; your dinner won't burn if you cook it 30 minutes longer. You can even serve the meal an hour or so early if your plans change.

For the best results with slow cooking, keep the following tips in mind:

- Slow cookers come in various sizes—from round to rectangular, and from 1- to 6-quart capacity. The smaller ones are best for vegetable side dishes or for keeping fondues warm.

- To find out the capacity of your slow cooker, fill it with water, and then measure the water in cups or quarts. Most recipes will specify the minimum size slow cooker needed.

- When cooking roasts, the shape may not fit your slow cooker. It's okay to cut the meat into 2 or 3 smaller pieces to fit your cooker.

- Make sure the slow cooker is at least half full for best results.

- Use the high and low heat settings to suit your schedule. Low allows you to cook a recipe all day, usually 8 to 12 hours. Recipes cook about twice as fast on the high setting. For example, a roast that cooks in 10 hours on low will be done in 5 hours on high.

- Avoid lifting the lid to peek; it will take another 20 minutes for the heat to return to the previous cooking temperature.

- Meats and stews cooked in a slow cooker retain more juices, so you need to add only a small amount of liquid in the beginning. Serve juicy meats with mashed potatoes, rice, or couscous to soak up the extra flavor.

- In addition to everyday entrées, use your slow cooker for serving warm dips and hot beverages.

Slow-Cooked Beef Pot Roast

Vegetable cooking spray

1 (3-pound) eye-of-round roast, trimmed

½ teaspoon ground pepper

1¼ cups water, divided

1 (0.8-ounce) package brown gravy mix with onions

1 teaspoon cornstarch

EXCHANGES

4 Very Lean Meat

POINTS

4

PER SERVING

162 Calories

1.9g Carbohydrate

4.8g Fat (1.7g saturated)

0.0g Fiber

26.0g Protein

65mg Cholesterol

192mg Sodium

4mg Calcium

2.4mg Iron

1. Coat a large nonstick skillet with cooking spray; place over medium-high heat. Sprinkle roast on all sides with pepper. Add roast to skillet, and cook until browned on all sides; place in a 3½- to 4-quart electric slow cooker coated with cooking spray.

2. Combine 1 cup water and gravy mix; pour over roast. Cover and cook on low heat 8 to 10 hours or on high heat 4 to 5 hours. Remove roast from sauce; cover roast, and keep warm.

3. Combine remaining ¼ cup water and cornstarch, stirring until smooth. Slowly stir cornstarch mixture into gravy in slow cooker. Pour mixture into a 1-quart microwave-safe glass measure, stirring until blended. Microwave at HIGH 2 minutes or until thickened, stirring after 1 minute. Serve roast with gravy. Yield: 12 servings.

Serve with roasted potatoes and carrots.

Long, slow cooking tenderizes lean cuts of meat. Other lean roasts you can substitute include round tip and sirloin.

Country Steak with Gravy

EXCHANGES
4 Very Lean Meat

POINTS
4

PER SERVING
165 Calories
3.4g Carbohydrate
4.7g Fat (1.7g saturated)
0.1g Fiber
26.9g Protein
65mg Cholesterol
409mg Sodium
9mg Calcium
2.7mg Iron

1 (12-ounce) jar fat-free beef-flavored gravy
1 teaspoon dried thyme
½ teaspoon ground pepper
¼ teaspoon garlic powder
Vegetable cooking spray
1½ pounds boneless top round steak (½ inch thick)

1. Combine gravy, thyme, pepper, and garlic powder in a 4-quart electric slow cooker coated with cooking spray.

2. Cut steak into serving-size pieces, and add to slow cooker; spoon gravy over steak to completely cover steak. Cover and cook on low heat 8 hours. Yield: 6 servings.

Serve with rice and glazed carrots.

> Jars of fat-free beef gravy and poultry gravy are great convenience products for low-fat cooking. However, they are higher in sodium than traditional canned or jarred gravies.

Southwest Meat Loaf (photo, page 176)

Vegetable cooking spray

2   pounds ground round

3   slices light sandwich bread, crumbled (1 cup)

1   cup chopped onion (about 1 medium)

½   cup fat-free egg substitute

¼   teaspoon salt

¼   teaspoon ground pepper

½   cup ketchup

½   cup thick and chunky salsa

EXCHANGES

4 Very Lean Meat

½ Starch

POINTS

4

PER SERVING

209 Calories

9.8g Carbohydrate

6.0g Fat (2.1g saturated)

1.1g Fiber

27.9g Protein

66mg Cholesterol

415mg Sodium

31mg Calcium

3.1mg Iron

1. Coat a 3½-quart electric slow cooker with cooking spray. Tear off two lengths of aluminum foil long enough to fit in bottom of slow cooker and extend 3 inches over each side of slow cooker. Fold each foil strip lengthwise to form 2-inch-wide strips. Arrange foil strips in a cross fashion in cooker, pressing strips in bottom of cooker and extending ends over sides of cooker.

2. Combine beef and next 5 ingredients; shape mixture into a loaf the shape of the slow cooker container. Place loaf in slow cooker over foil strips. (Foil strips become "handles" to remove meat loaf from slow cooker.) Make a shallow indention on top of meat loaf. Combine ketchup and salsa; pour over meat loaf.

3. Cover and cook on low heat 8 hours or on high heat 3½ to 4 hours. Use foil strips to lift meat loaf from cooker. Let meat loaf stand 10 minutes before serving. Yield: 8 servings.

Serve with mashed potatoes and steamed green beans.

This meat loaf recipe is especially good served with the Mashed Parsley Potatoes on page 165.

Cranberry Pork Roast

EXCHANGES

3 Lean Meat

1 Starch

POINTS

6

PER SERVING

252 Calories

17.0g Carbohydrate

9.3g Fat (3.0g saturated)

0.0g Fiber

23.5g Protein

68mg Cholesterol

169mg Sodium

17mg Calcium

1.1mg Iron

Vegetable cooking spray

1   (3-pound) boneless pork loin roast, trimmed

1   (16-ounce) can jellied whole-berry cranberry sauce

¼   cup steak sauce

1   tablespoon brown sugar

1   teaspoon prepared mustard

2   tablespoons water

2   tablespoons cornstarch

1. Coat a large nonstick skillet with cooking spray; place over medium-high heat. Add roast; cook until browned on all sides. Place roast in a 4- to 5-quart electric slow cooker coated with cooking spray.

2. Combine cranberry sauce and next 3 ingredients; pour over roast. Cover and cook on low heat 8 hours or on high heat 4 to 5 hours. Remove roast from sauce; cover and keep warm.

3. Combine water and cornstarch, stirring until smooth. Slowly stir cornstarch mixture into sauce in slow cooker. Pour mixture into a 1-quart microwave-safe glass measure. Microwave at HIGH 2 minutes, stirring after 1 minute. Serve roast with gravy. Yield: 12 servings.

Serve with couscous and steamed broccoli.

You don't have to brown the roast before putting it in the slow cooker. However, browning the outside of the roast first adds a rich caramelized flavor to the meat.

Picante Pork Chops

8   (6-ounce) bone-in center-cut pork loin chops

Vegetable cooking spray

1   (16-ounce) jar thick and chunky picante sauce

1. Trim fat from pork chops. Coat a large skillet with cooking spray, and place over medium-high heat until hot. Add chops; cook until browned on both sides.

2. Pour one-fourth of picante sauce into a 3½- to 4-quart electric slow cooker coated with cooking spray; add chops. Top with remaining picante sauce. Cover and cook on low heat 10 hours or on high heat 3 to 4 hours. Reserve 1 cup sauce. Serve 2 tablespoons sauce over each chop. Yield: 8 servings.

Serve with rice and steamed zucchini.

To remove excess fat from the sauce, drop an ice cube into the sauce, and remove the ice with a slotted spoon. The hardened fat will cling to the ice cube.

EXCHANGES

2 Lean Meat

POINTS

3

PER SERVING

119 Calories

3.0g Carbohydrate

4.7g Fat (1.6g saturated)

0.4g Fiber

15.2g Protein

41mg Cholesterol

273mg Sodium

3mg Calcium

0.5mg Iron

Chill-Breaker Turkey Chili

EXCHANGES

2 Very Lean Meat

2 Starch

POINTS

4

PER SERVING

268 Calories

31.3g Carbohydrate

2.5g Fat (1.0g saturated)

8.0g Fiber

21.0g Protein

45mg Cholesterol

463mg Sodium

13mg Calcium

0.9mg Iron

Vegetable cooking spray

1   pound ground turkey breast

1   cup frozen chopped onion

1   (8-ounce) can no-salt-added tomato sauce

1   (30-ounce) can chili-hot beans, undrained

1   (1.25-ounce) package mild chili seasoning mix

1. Coat a Dutch oven with cooking spray; add turkey and onion, and place over high heat. Cook, stirring constantly, until turkey crumbles and onion is tender.

2. Add tomato sauce, beans, and seasoning mix to turkey mixture; stir well. Pour mixture into a 3½- to 4-quart electric slow cooker coated with cooking spray. Cover and cook on low heat 8 to 10 hours or on high heat 4 to 5 hours. Yield: 6 (1-cup) servings.

Serve with cornbread.

To save time you can add the ground turkey to the slow cooker without cooking the turkey first. The texture of the cooked turkey will be a bit softer, but we liked it both ways.

Recipe Index

No-Cook Recipes

Tips Index

Acknowledgments

Cyclamen Studio, Inc., Berkeley, CA
Daisy Hill, Louisville, KY
E&M Glass, Cheshire, UK
Eigen Arts, Inc., Jersey City, NJ
Jill Rosenwald, Boston, MA
Pillivyt-Franmara, Salinas, CA
Smyer Glass, Benicia, CA

Union Street Glass, Oakland, CA
Vietri, Hillsborough, NC

Sources of Nutrient Analysis Data:
Computrition, Inc., Chatsworth, CA, and
information provided by food manufacturers

Metric Equivalents

The recipes that appear in this cookbook use the standard United States method for measuring liquid and dry or solid ingredients (teaspoons, tablespoons, and cups). The information in the following charts is provided to help cooks outside the U.S. successfully use these recipes. All equivalents are approximate.

Equivalents for Different Types of Ingredients

A standard cup measure of a dry or solid ingredient will vary in weight depending on the type of ingredient. A standard cup of liquid is the same volume for any type of liquid. Use the following chart when converting standard cup measures to grams (weight) or milliliters (volume).

Standard Cup	Fine Powder (ex. flour)	Grain (ex. rice)	Granular (ex. sugar)	Liquid Solids (ex. butter)	Liquid (ex. milk)
1	140 g	150 g	190 g	200 g	240 ml
¾	105 g	113 g	143 g	150 g	180 ml
⅔	93 g	100 g	125 g	133 g	160 ml
½	70 g	75 g	95 g	100 g	120 ml
⅓	47 g	50 g	63 g	67 g	80 ml
¼	35 g	38 g	48 g	50 g	60 ml
⅛	18 g	19 g	24 g	25 g	30 ml

Dry Ingredients by Weight

(To convert ounces to grams, multiply the number of ounces by 30.)

1 oz	=	¹⁄₁₆ lb	=	30 g
4 oz	=	¼ lb	=	120 g
8 oz	=	½ lb	=	240 g
12 oz	=	¾ lb	=	360 g
16 oz	=	1 lb	=	480 g

Length

(To convert inches to centimeters, multiply the number of inches by 2.5.)

1 in	=			=	2.5 cm		
6 in	=	½ ft		=	15 cm		
12 in	=	1 ft		=	30 cm		
36 in	=	3 ft	=	1 yd	=	90 cm	
40 in	=			=	100 cm	=	1 m

Liquid Ingredients by Volume

¼ tsp						1 ml
½ tsp						2 ml
1 tsp						5 ml
3 tsp	=	1 tbls		=	½ fl oz	=	15 ml
		2 tbls	= ⅛ cup	=	1 fl oz	=	30 ml
		4 tbls	= ¼ cup	=	2 fl oz	=	60 ml
		5⅓ tbls	= ⅓ cup	=	3 fl oz	=	80 ml
		8 tbls	= ½ cup	=	4 fl oz	=	120 ml
		10⅔ tbls	= ⅔ cup	=	5 fl oz	=	160 ml
		12 tbls	= ¾ cup	=	6 fl oz	=	180 ml
		16 tbls	= 1 cup	=	8 fl oz	=	240 ml
		1 pt	= 2 cups	=	16 fl oz	=	480 ml
		1 qt	= 4 cups	=	32 fl oz	=	960 ml
					33 fl oz	=	1000 ml = 1 liter

Cooking/Oven Temperatures

	Fahrenheit	Celsius	Gas Mark
Freeze Water	32° F	0° C	
Room Temperature	68° F	20° C	
Boil Water	212° F	100° C	
Bake	325° F	160° C	3
	350° F	180° C	4
	375° F	190° C	5
	400° F	200° C	6
	425° F	220° C	7
	450° F	230° C	8
Broil			Grill

Calorie-Burning Activities

The numbers on this chart reflect how many calories are burned per minute by people of various weights during specific activities.

	Weight			
	120 lbs.	140 lbs.	160 lbs.	180 lbs.
Activity	Calories burned per minute			
Basketball	7.5	8.8	10.0	11.3
Bowling	1.2	1.4	1.6	1.9
Cycling (10 m.p.h.)	5.5	6.4	7.3	8.2
Dancing (aerobic)	7.4	8.6	9.8	11.1
Dancing (social)	2.9	3.3	3.7	4.2
Gardening	5.0	5.9	6.7	7.5
Golf (power cart)	2.1	2.5	2.8	3.2
Golf (pull/carry clubs)	4.6	5.4	6.2	7.0
Hiking	4.5	5.2	6.0	6.7
Jogging	9.3	10.8	12.4	13.9
Running	11.4	13.2	15.1	17.0
Sitting quietly	1.2	1.3	1.5	1.7
Skating (ice and roller)	5.9	6.9	7.9	8.8
Skiing (cross-country)	7.5	8.8	10.0	11.3
Skiing (water and downhill)	5.7	6.6	7.6	8.5
Swimming (crawl, moderate pace)	7.8	9.0	10.3	11.6
Tennis	6.0	6.9	7.9	8.9
Walking (moderate pace)	6.5	7.6	8.7	9.7
Weight training	6.6	7.6	8.7	9.8

Reprinted with permission from the American Council on Exercise from ACE Fit Facts.

Handy Substitutions

Ingredient Needed	Substitute

Baking Products

Ingredient Needed	Substitute
1 cup self-rising flour	1 cup all-purpose flour, 1 teaspoon baking powder, and ½ teaspoon salt
1 cup cake flour	1 cup minus 2 tablespoons all-purpose flour
1 cup all-purpose flour	1 cup plus 2 tablespoons cake flour
1 cup powdered sugar	1 cup sugar and 1 tablespoon cornstarch (processed in food processor)
1 cup honey	1¼ cups sugar and ¼ cup water
1 teaspoon baking powder	¼ teaspoon baking soda and ½ teaspoon cream of tartar
1 tablespoon cornstarch	2 tablespoons all-purpose flour
1 tablespoon tapioca	1½ tablespoons all-purpose flour
½ cup chopped pecans	½ cup regular oats, toasted (in baked products)
1 ounce or square unsweetened chocolate	3 tablespoons cocoa and 1 tablespoon butter or margarine

Eggs and Dairy Products

Ingredient Needed	Substitute
2 large eggs	3 small eggs
1 cup fat-free milk	½ cup evaporated skimmed milk and ½ cup water
1 cup plain yogurt	1 cup buttermilk
1 cup nonfat sour cream	1 cup nonfat yogurt and 1 tablespoon cornstarch (for cooking)

Vegetable Products

Ingredient Needed	Substitute
1 pound fresh mushrooms, sliced	1 (8-ounce) can sliced mushrooms, drained, or 3 ounces dried
1 medium onion, chopped	1 tablespoon instant minced onion or 1 tablespoon onion powder
3 tablespoons chopped shallots	2½ tablespoons chopped onion and 1 teaspoon chopped garlic

Seasoning Products

Ingredient Needed	Substitute
1 tablespoon chopped fresh herbs	1 teaspoon dried herbs or ¼ teaspoon powdered herbs
1 clove garlic	⅛ teaspoon garlic powder or minced dried garlic or 1 teaspoon bottled minced garlic
1 tablespoon dried orange peel	1½ teaspoons orange extract or 1 tablespoon grated fresh orange rind
1 teaspoon ground allspice	½ teaspoon ground cinnamon and ½ teaspoon ground cloves
1 teaspoon pumpkin pie spice	½ teaspoon ground cinnamon, ¼ teaspoon ground ginger, ⅛ teaspoon ground allspice, and ⅛ teaspoon ground nutmeg

Alcohol

Ingredient Needed	Substitute
2 tablespoons amaretto	¼ to ½ teaspoon almond extract
2 tablespoons sherry or bourbon	1 to 2 teaspoons vanilla extract
¼ cup Marsala	¼ cup dry white wine and 1 teaspoon brandy
¼ cup or more white wine	Equal measure of apple juice (in sweet dishes) or reduced-sodium chicken broth (in savory dishes)
¼ cup or more red wine	Equal measure of red grape juice or cranberry juice